P9-DBP-559

By Herbert Block

STRAIGHT HERBLOCK

HERBLOCK'S SPECIAL FOR TODAY

HERBLOCK'S HERE AND NOW

THE HERBLOCK BOOK

Herbert Block

STRAIGHT HERBLOCK

Simon and Schuster
New York

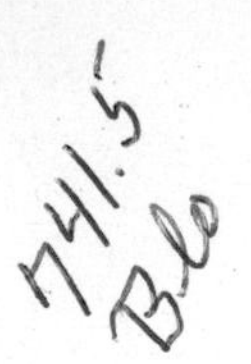

PUBLISHED BY SIMON AND SCHUSTER. INC.
ROCKEFELLER CENTER, 630 FIFTH AVENUE, NEW YORK 20, N. Y.

FIRST PRINTING

Most of the cartoons in this book appeared originally in the Washington *Post* and were distributed by the Hall Syndicate.

LIBRARY OF CONGRESS CATALOG CARD NUMBER: 64-24335
MANUFACTURED IN THE UNITED STATES OF AMERICA
DESIGNED BY HELEN BARROW
PRINTED BY MAHONY & ROESE, NEW YORK
BOUND BY H. WOLFF, NEW YORK

To my brother Richard M. Block;
and to Jane Asher, Helen Barrow
and Jean Bonieskie

Contents

1. Memory Lane to Campaign Trail

"WHAT IS PAST IS PROLOGUE," reads the line from Shakespeare on the Archives Building in Washington; but past office-holders have a hard time confining themselves to prologues and keep trying to get into the act.

Whatever the fate of old campaigners, old campaigns and old election nights live on, sometimes even longer than the clean-up-the-government campaign posters cling to fences and telephone poles.

David Brinkley wrote that "Elections are no fun anymore"* now that early statistics are fed into electronic devices that grind and whir and come up with the probable election result even before the polls are closed. And many citizens who used to enjoy delicious suspense and neighborly speculation on an election night have become angrier at the electronic machines than they ever were at the old political machines. Eventually there may be an anti-electronic-machine revolt, in which voters will go late to the polls just to overthrow the computing machines and restore good old-fashioned honest uncertainty.

Perhaps the reason for maintaining the electoral college has been to keep an element of uncertainty about who "unpledged electors" will vote for and who, regardless of majority vote, will actually be elected President. I can

*Look magazine, July 14, 1964.

"WE'RE ALMOST READY TO TAKE OFF AGAIN."

11/24/60

"WE'RE GONNA HAVE TO GET THAT THING FIXED."

12/18/60

think of no other justification for this outdated piece of political machinery. I hope it will be scrapped before it can ever again surprise an unhappy majority in a state or in the nation.

The new electronic election prediction machines I don't know about. It can be said for them that if they are fallible, at least they are not official. But where there is no overwhelming trend, I for one continue to watch and listen to all the returns, and will probably wind up with ulcers from worrying through election nights while others flip off their sets early and go to bed. I like to think there are still a few surprises left in elections, even if there do not seem to be many left in nominating conventions. And sometimes there are.

In 1960 some of the state elections hung in the balance for days and weeks; and the Presidential election held surprises and uncertainties for those of us who stayed on past the early prediction—which eventually proved correct.

Even more surprising than election returns are the post-election returns I sometimes get. For example, after I had sat before the TV all night, chewing my nails over that 1960 election and finally giving a large sigh of relief at the result, it was a little unnerving to me to hear afterward—in fact for days, weeks and months afterward—expressions of sympathy that the election had come out as I had hoped it would.

"Too bad, old boy, about the election—" people would tell me, "—you know—losing Nixon." The "loss" of this political figure, and of the administration he had been associated with, was mentioned constantly. At one cocktail party shortly after that election, a lady who had listened to the fifth person commiserate with me on losing that Presidential possibility, endeared herself to me for life by asking, "Why do you suppose he *did* all those cartoons about Mr. Nixon?"

The impression seems to be that, like the fellow in *My Fair Lady*, I develop an attachment for a face to which I've grown accustomed. But I'm not really one to have my head turned by an unpretty face—or an unpretty character; and I'd just as soon not have to keep turning my hand to them either.

There is always "cartoon material" as long as there are public figures and differing views. There are always people on "the other side" of questions—usually some in both parties. In the

"THE OUTCOME WAS, OF COURSE, INEVITABLE—"

11/8/60

"NOW, WITH JUST ANOTHER SMALL SWITCH—"

11/10/60

"WILL THE REAL RICHARD NIXON PLEASE STAND UP?"
6/9/60

"YOU SAY KENNEDY IS YOUNG AND IMPULSIVE AND SPENDS MONEY. TELL ME MORE ABOUT THIS TERRIBLE MAN."
10/28/60

GREAT DEBATE
10/2/60

"A LITTLE CLOSER–NOT TOO CLOSE–SMILE–THAT'S IT."
7/27/60

"HAS THERE BEEN ANY PRESSURE ON YOU, GOVERNOR?"
7/19/60

"WHICH FACE AND WHAT OPINIONS WILL DICK PUT ON NEXT? TUNE IN AGAIN..."
10/16/60

unlikely event that I should ever approve of everything an Administration did (which I never have) there would still be "material" in Congress and elsewhere. There was a cartoonist named Nast who, while reluctant to criticize Administrations in Washington, found useful employment for his pen working on the Tweed Ring.

For anyone who has definite opinions on a number of subjects, there is never a shortage of issues or of characters—and as far as I'm concerned never a time when it's not pleasant to see an issue settled properly or have someone I'm *pro* defeat someone I'm *anti*.

But I have as little hope of convincing anyone of this as I have of convincing people that reprinted cartoons are not necessarily the "best" ones—or of the fact that I don't use suggestions for cartoons. And the last time I mentioned *that* in a little article, I got twice as many "idea" letters as usual the following week, because all anyone remembered was that there was something in the article about this cartoonist and "ideas"—and he'd probably like some.

I think it was the late Eugene Meyer who said, when reporters sought his reaction to the departure from government of a man who had long feuded with him, "I do not feel lonely."

By now I'm used to having people console me when unfavorite politicians leave office; and I've almost given up explaining that I do not feel lonely without them. I am merely grateful to the few who understand that I am not in this line of work for the joy of drawing faces—particularly some of the same old ones that I wish would go away.

If in some way the happy day should come when there would be no nuclear weapons to fear and no possibility of war in the world ever again, I know that some kind, well-meaning person would come running to share my "misfortune" and to say, "Golly, it's too bad you won't have your old A-bomb character to draw any more. Tough luck!"

All I ask is that while they are expressing their condolences over the loss of the last subject, the last issue and the last character, they don't let their tears fall on the wet ink of the cartoon I'm doing on The Next One. ■

"FOLKS—WAIT—LISTEN—"

11/2/60

"MIRROR, MIRROR, ON THE WALL, WHO'S THE FAIREST ONE OF ALL?"

1/2/60

"SELDOM HAS A CANDIDATE HAD SO MUCH EXPERIENCE AT NOT BEING RESPONSIBLE FOR DECISIONS."

8/25/60

"OUR PRESTIGE WAS NEVER HIGHER."

10/12/60

"FASTER, DAMMIT!"

10/25/60

2. Economics and All That Stuff

We are living in a period when the economy of the nation is extremely complicated and when unemployment statistics, studied closely, show that few economists are out of work.

The entrails of stock tickers are examined, along with other auguries, like the consumer price index, carloadings, production capacity, and so on.

With no credentials except a few sales slips, which I can never find when I need them, I would like to add my bit to the general confusion and call attention to what the professional economists have overlooked. They've studied production time, but have they ever considered the non-production time that we consumers put in looking for deliveries from stores, waiting for shipments that never come in? Let us forget for a moment the Gross National Product (GNP) and consider the Consumer Waiting Time (CWT).

You purchase a washing machine at a store and ask when it will be delivered. In your particular part of town, which is easily accessible, they can't guarantee anything this week, but it might come the following week, either on a Tuesday or on a Thursday—wait a minute, Thursday is a holiday—either next Tuesday or the Tuesday after.

You ask if they couldn't be more definite, close in on a single day. And finally they agree to make it this Tuesday, and they are even willing to bracket the time of delivery. It will be between 7:00 A.M. and midnight.

After a useless vigil, the purchase arrives on a Wednesday, at noon, and is taken back to the warehouse because nobody is home. But it finally comes again on the following Friday at 6:00 A.M., after you've worked till 1:00 A.M. the night before, because lucky you happened to be first on the list that morning—the delivery list that nobody gets to see, and which is operated as a kind of lottery.

In an era of walkie-talkies, two-way-radio cabs, telephones on street corners and in automobiles, of IBM machines, and maps with all kinds of colored pins on them, nobody can phone a customer to say "Here we come" or "Sorry we can't make it today." Nobody knows when a truck will pick up a piece of merchandise and when it will make a delivery. These delivery trucks, like a fleet of ghost shops on wheels, pull out of their garage ports each morning in a heavy fog and return at night in another heavy fog. And the spectral drivers speak to nobody, and nobody speaks to them.

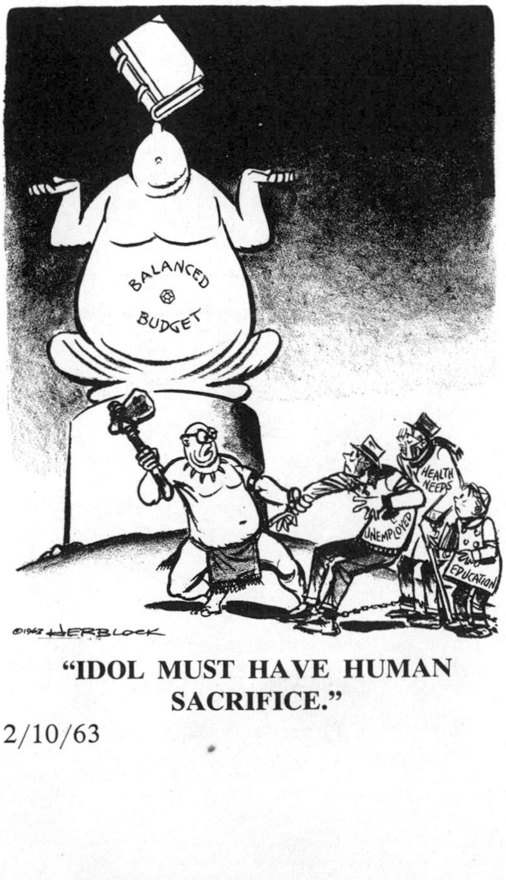

"IDOL MUST HAVE HUMAN SACRIFICE."

2/10/63

"GOT TO KEEP THINGS BALANCED, YOU KNOW."
12/24/58

"LOOK OUT FOR THAT DITCH!"
3/10/59

"I DON'T KNOW WHY EVERYTHING HAS TO KEEP CHANGING. WHEN I WAS A YOUNG MAN–"
12/8/58

A heavy fog also permeates much of what goes on in the rest of the economic field, and it particularly surrounds many of the politicians who keep talking about it.

I will not here go into a detailed discussion of the Balanced Budget, which gets into the field of Religion. I always felt that President Eisenhower was entitled to his belief in this Faith, even though he didn't practice it. And while I didn't agree with them, I respected his views on the Economic Hereafter, which was obviously more important than anything in the material and prosaic present. With so many short-sighted people concerned about today's children, and even our children's children, it has been good to have a Gen. Eisenhower always thinking and speaking about our children's *grand*children—or, more specifically, George M. Humphrey's children's grandchildren, who are going to have all that money to worry about and pay taxes on.

Concerned as so many of us have been with seeing that there is still a livable world and a decent civilization for future generations (which we hope will arrive safely and not be affected by nuclear mutations), how many people have bothered to think about the unborn tax problems of those unborn tykes—or grand-tykes?

On a related subject, I have also long been impressed with the vision and broadmindedness of those people who are against spending the small percentage of national income that goes for welfare measures because, they tell us, Marx or Lenin or somebody was reported to have said somewhere that we would be "bled white" by expenditures. Some of us hold to narrow

"WE'RE CLEVERLY FOOLING THE RUSSIANS BY ACTING AS IF OUR COUNTRY WERE BANKRUPT."

3/16/59

views that men like Marx and Lenin guessed wrong; and that, in any case, we should merely be concerned with what seems best for the U.S. We can well feel shamed in our parochial view by those people who are more anti-Communist than anybody, but who are big enough to accept as gospel anything supposedly said by Marx or Lenin, or even some present-day Communist, so long as it fits their own philosophies.

In the bright lexicon of cash, the greatest phrase has been *Free Enterprise*, which is itself a term so flexibly free that it can mean anything anybody wants it to.

To some industries, for example, it is free enterprise to get whatever the traffic will bear, with the government minding its own business and merely seeing to it that the industries get fat contracts and are protected by the government against any risk of loss.

Jimmy Hoffa had his own brand of free enterprise, which seemed to provide the maximum freedom and enterprise for Mr. Hoffa.

The American Medical Association—or the witch doctors who engage in political malpractice in its name—has *its* ideas about free enterprise, which have involved the freedom to spend doctors' dues to fight a public health insurance plan under which patients would continue to choose their own doctors, and the doctors would get paid. Many of these same AMA members, meeting in San Francisco in 1964, endorsed a Republican Presidential candidate who protested bitterly against unions spending members' money in politics.

"CUSTOM-BUILT...POWER STEERING ...FINGERTIP CONTROL."

7/8/61

Economics, business and finance get a little complicated here. What you have to understand is that it's all right for the government to insure a man's savings deposits against the possibility of a bank failure. But it's wrong for the government to insure the same man against a health failure, which will not only wipe out his savings, but will do so just when he's least able to earn money to replace them. Everything clear now?

The head of U.S. Steel, in April 1962, demonstrated *his* idea of free enterprise, which consisted of a big business doing as it pleased after the President of the United States had just helped in negotiations to keep down union demands. He dropped by the White House of an evening to mention casually that, by the way, he was boosting prices. Just like that! Don't call us, we'll call you.

For not accepting this idea of the government's role in our national life, Mr. Kennedy got the tag of anti-business. But, as others have noted, the state of business is not necessarily related to the business state of mind.

On hearing the news of the Kennedy-Big Steel set-to, one man said (according to an article later that year in *Esquire*) that the U.S. economy was in a peck of trouble because of poor judgment among business leaders, and that there was a conflict of interest going on right now in every big corporation that gave stock options to its management. The interviewer went on to quote him:

> Ever since the war, these business fellers have been payin' dividends instead of putting money into new plants and equipment. And now they're crying to the government for tax relief so they can get enough money to modernize their plants. They're so far behind! I ask you—why did management in steel, oil, and railroads choose dividends and stock splits over modernization? I'll tell you —it was because those fellers have more in-

"UH–PERHAPS WE SHOULD HAVE A CONSULTATION."

5/24/62

"QUICK–BOIL LOTS OF WATER."

5/11/62

"AND HERE'S THE REPORT ON YOUR LATEST CHECKUP AT WALTER REED HOSPITAL."

3/23/60

"PERHAPS SOME DAY A KIND OF VOLUNTARY PROGRAM FOR–UH–VOLUNTARY ILLNESSES."

4/1/60

terest in their own pocketbooks than they have in running a prudent operation. Stock options are supposed to be an incentive, but they've brought us to the point where now big business has to have more profits and more tax breaks and more depreciation allowances just to compete with old Europe. It's funny, isn't it?

If you can imagine a politician talking that way, *there's* a fellow that Big Business might well have taken after as being really *anti*. But they didn't, perhaps because he sounded too radical to deserve attention. The fellow who said those things at the time of the 1962 steel crisis was a Midwestern businessman and sometime politician named Alf Landon.

President Johnson fared better than his predecessors with most businessmen, possibly because the Johnsons had some business properties of their own, and because the President had turned off those unused closet lights in the White House. But some economy advocates felt it was a dirty trick when President Johnson and Secretary McNamara actually practiced economy by cutting needless and costly defense establishments.

In May 1959 I did the cartoon of possible-candidate Lyndon Johnson standing precariously on two horses. And in 1964, there he is, actually riding a couple of somewhat similar horses.

In this survey of business, finance, economics, and whatnot, there is one other matter I don't want to miss. That is the debt ceiling, which Congress raises and lowers with the national debt in a ritual that is supposed to ward off the Evil Spirit of Spending. Somebody has

4/12/62

"THE LIGHTS ARE GOING OUT ALL OVER THE COUNTRY."

4/28/64

observed that the attempt to keep down the debt by means of a "debt ceiling" is comparable to trying to raise and lower an elevator by grabbing the little arrow on the indicator above the elevator door—a comparison that is quite apt.

You don't see those old elevator indicators much anymore, and I miss them. What they have above the store elevator doors now is a couple of little ground-glass arrows, one pointing up and the other down. At intervals there is a *ping* and one of these lights goes on. But in between times you have no idea where the elevator is. If it's stuck somewhere, a fellow can spend hours watching a couple of unlit glass arrows. Do you know how much Consumer Waiting Time is today going into elevators-without-indicators alone?

Now, another thing about those stores . . . ■

"IT DOESN'T HOLD HIM DOWN, BUT IT ANNOYS HELL OUT OF HIM."
6/14/62

"IF HE AIN'T RUNNING, HE'S SURE DOING SOME FANCY RIDING."
5/1/59

"MONOPOLIST!"
1/23/64

"THAT KENNEDY SEEMS LIKE A PRETTY NICE SORT—FOR A FELLOW WHO BELIEVES IN GOVERNMENT, THAT IS."
5/1/62

"SAY, HOW COME YOU DON'T LIKE THIS GUY?"
8/15/62

"STOP HIM—HE'S DIGGING A HOLE."
1/23/63

"REMINDS ME OF THAT CRAZY IDEA OF HENRY FORD'S THAT YOU CAN MAKE MORE SELLING AT LOWER PRICES."
1/20/63

"WELL, THAT WAS A HELL OF A SHORT DAY!"
4/15/62

"WHY DON'T WE HAVE THE THRIFTY BUDGETS OF BEN FRANKLIN'S DAY?"
1/18/63

"AH, DYING IS HARD FOR BOTH OF US."

6/12/62

"I HELP TO SUPPORT THE ESTABLISHMENTS I HAVE MENTIONED; THEY COST ENOUGH, AND THOSE WHO ARE BADLY OFF MUST GO THERE."

11/29/61 —*A Christmas Carol*

"THERE, NOW, YOU'LL BE SOUND AS A DOLLAR–THOUGH NOT QUITE AS IMPORTANT, OF COURSE."
5/5/60

"NOW WOULD YOU ALSO CARE TO SIGN UP FOR OPTIONAL SOCIAL SECURITY, OPTIONAL POLICE AND FIRE DEPARTMENTS, OPTIONAL ARMED FORCES..."
4/24/60

SPLIT-LEVEL LIVING
3/9/60

"WHY DON'T YOU SOAR?"
3/15/63

"CAREFUL YOU DON'T SET THE WHOLE DORMITORY ON FIRE."
5/10/61

"TAKE UP THY BED AND WALK."
3/5/63

"GUESS WE MADE IT AGAIN, I HOPE."
4/14/64

"ONWARD!––HELP! I'VE BEEN STABBED!"
12/13/63

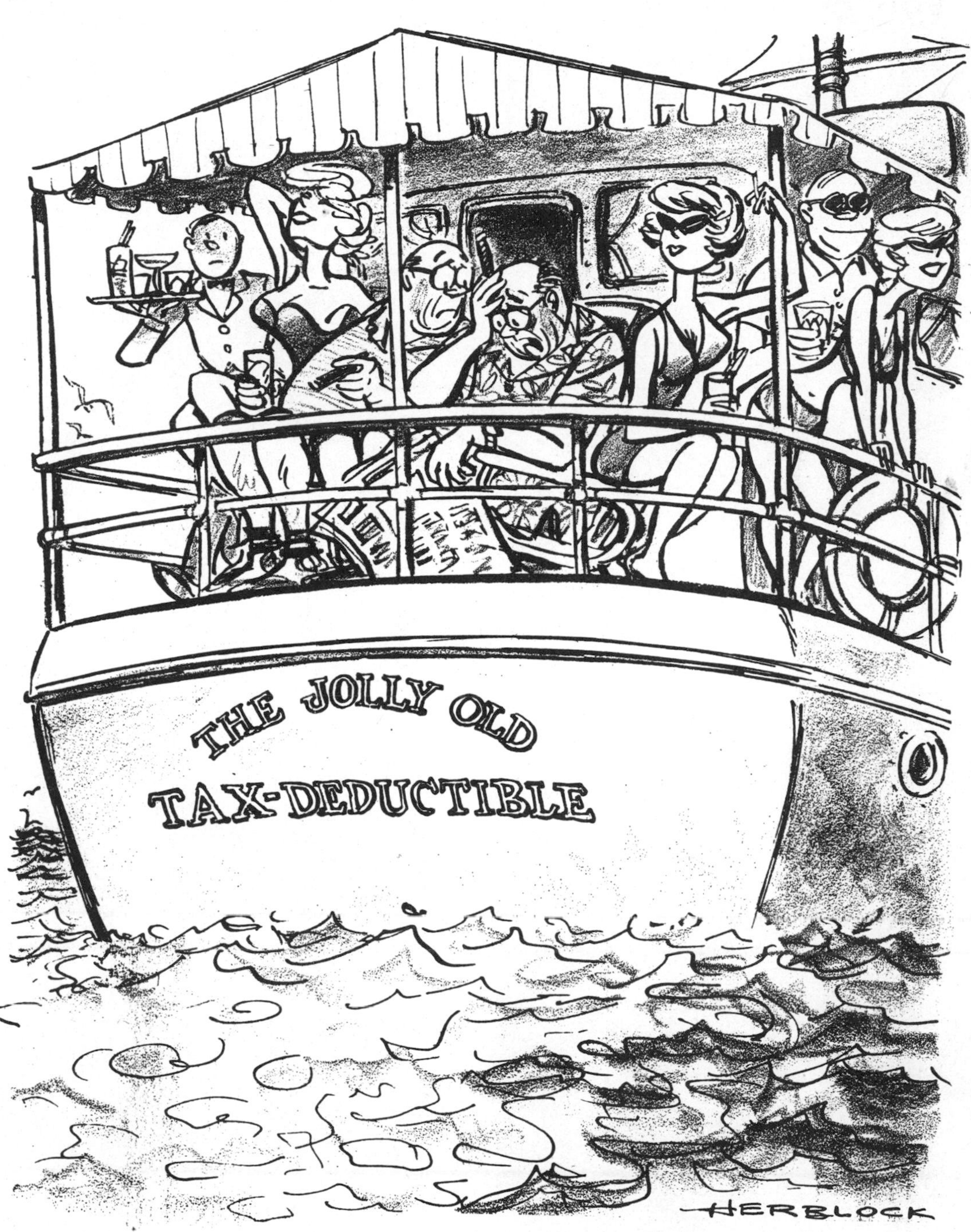

"PRIVATE ENTERPRISE HAS BEEN DEALT ANOTHER BLOW. THE GOVERNMENT WANTS US TO PAY FOR THIS OURSELVES."
5/12/61

"IT LOOKS AS IF WE'LL HAVE A GOOD CORN CROP TOO."

8/12/59

"WHOA THERE, HORSIE– I SAY, WHOA!"

3/8/59

"CAN'T TAKE ANY CHANCE OF BEING BLOWN OVERBOARD."

1/26/59

"IT'S TOO NICE A SUIT TO ALTER– JUST SCRUNCH DOWN AND WALK LIKE A CRIPPLE."

5/3/59

3. Heads of State and Vice Versa

It's a long time since I went abroad, and most of the French atmosphere I get these days comes from travels down the street to local restaurants whose menus combine a little Gallic with the garlic—and which are designed to be as illegible as possible.

This they accomplish by a three-ply ploy. *(1)* the menu, but of course, is in French. *(2)* It is not enough that the menu should be *printed* in French—it has to be written, usually in a kind of double-talk script that looks like the most carefully written hand but does not resemble actual writing. And for a clincher *(3)* these written French menus are run off on a hectograph and printed in the closest thing possible to invisible ink. By throwing away the first 200 copies of the menu that are run off, the restaurateur is able to produce a shade of pale lavender that can scarcely be seen, even at an outdoor table at lunchtime. At dinner, which is by candlelight, a resident optometrist could make a killing.

What the menu requires is a French code expert with X-ray eyes.

This restaurantship, which patronizes the patron, is designed to intimidate him into taking what is more or less plainly marked *spécialité de la maison,* which is what they are pushing that day. The desired effect is to have the customer take without complaint, and at

MAJORITY OF ONE

11/28/62

"YOU MIGHT SAY THAT THEY SEE I-TO-I."

3/24/60

"TELL ME, AS ONE OLD SOLDIER TO ANOTHER, HOW DOES IT FEEL ACTUALLY TO RUN A GOVERNMENT?"

4/22/60

high prices, the modest portion of whatever-it-is they serve him, leave a big tip to show that he's not a bumpkin, and be grateful if the waiter does not sneer at him on the way out.

What places like that are doing is creating ill-will for France, that's what they're doing—and strengthening the conviction that the French will rob you and spit in your eye.

I must rise to the defense of General de Gaulle (formerly known as La Belle France) and point out that he should bear no part of the blame for the confusion and ill-will created by those American French restaurants that go in for le grand price and haughty cuisine. They were doing that sort of thing before he came to power. Furthermore, he has proved himself well able to create confusion and ill-will entirely on his own, and with no need for help from any confederates over here.

He looms in this section among heads of governments, and a very high and large head he has, too. It is unlikely that he would care much for most of the company in which I've placed him, since, after all, he's the only one who is a complete nation and a great power all by himself.

How can one help having mixed feelings about this strange character? In World War II, the stature he achieved by sheer force of personality—without troops and without having headed any government or any victorious army—is breathtaking. That he should have felt rebuffed and injured that Roosevelt and Churchill, who *did* have the position and power and means and responsibility for winning the war, did not treat him as a precise equal is equally incredible in its effrontery.

His postwar leadership, beginning with his overcoming the perils presented by some of the former underground factions—formidable! His failure to observe the twentieth anniversary of D-day, waiting instead to observe the anniversary of the entrance into Paris which he was given the honor of leading, may have been a small thing in itself, but it also seemed small in spirit. That kind of thing makes you wonder if a man who really believed he was the head of a great power would feel obliged to act in such fashion.

If there is a de Gaulle motto, it might well be: *In defeat, unbearable; in victory, insufferable.*

"IT'S CALLED 'GRAND DESIGN.'"
3/17/63

"LOOK, EVERYBODY, I'M NOT PAYING ANY ATTENTION."
6/23/63

1/31/60

12/22/60

At times I've been tempted to draw him as a centaur—a unique, a mythological being—a magnificent figure of a man combined with what is unmistakably the rear end of a horse.

Perhaps, as someone said, he is a great man of the 19th and the 21st centuries. But a man whose idea of Europe seemed rather exclusively a French-German coalition—who opposed a nuclear test ban treaty and showed himself insensitive to fallout dangers—who sneered at "that thing," the United Nations, in which he declined to pay his peacekeeping dues . . . he must have missed out on something important about the 20th century; and however tall, has not shown the full stature he might have reached.

He can turn up his nose if he chooses and look away from the drawings of Macmillan—the unflappable Mac—who stood up to Common Market opposition at home only to have the market door slammed in his face by de Gaulle. One of these pictures, drawn when Macmillan expressed himself on behalf of joining with Europe in this enterprise, has him appearing quite continental. Just how continental some in Mac's government were, we did not realize till the Profumo affair. Whatever else *that* did, it certainly should have obliterated the idea that the British were stuffy fellows, spending their time sitting around stuffy clubs.

There are a few other heads here, too, from both East and West—some long heads, some strong heads, some soreheads, and some inevitable warheads. There is even a pair of headstones.

There are also a few examples of heads-togetherness that may seem at first glance surprising. But the so-called "extreme left" and "extreme right" are on opposite sides of the hall in the same anti-democratic house, and it's not astonishing that they should find their way into each other's beds. ■

"FRIGHTFULLY SORRY, REALLY."
6/19/63

"PERHAPS MAC MIGHT BE GLAD TO HAVE SOME OLD, TIRED BLOOD IN THE GOVERNMENT AGAIN."
6/7/63

"IT DOES TAKE AWAY A LITTLE FROM THE GRANDEUR."
3/27/63

"MARVELOUS! NOW WHO CAN WE TRUST TO BE IN CHARGE OF IT?"
2/16/60

"NATURALLY, I WOULD HAVE TO CONSIDER CAREFULLY ANY LIMITATIONS IN THE ATMOSPHERE OR OUTER SPACE."

8/1/63

"I CAN BE CONTINENTAL, Y'KNOW."
8/3/61

"COME IN—WE PUT OUT THE WELCOME MOAT FOR YOU."
12/18/62

"MY VOICES TELL ME TO DRIVE OUT THE BRITISH IF IT TAKES ALL OF THE 15TH CENTURY."
1/15/63

"BRITAIN IS NOT YET READY TO JOIN EUROPE."

1/25/63

"AFTER ALL, I HAVE MY PRIDE TOO, YOU KNOW."

8/15/63

"WHAT DO YOU MEAN, I CAN'T TAKE IT WITH ME?"

4/30/63

"I DON'T KNOW HOW *YOU* FEEL, BUT IT'S MAKING *ME* NERVOUS."

1/24/64

"I ALWAYS SAY THREE HEADS ARE BETTER THAN ONE."

6/20/61

"NOW?"

11/7/62

NILE BARGE

5/14/64

"ALL ARE GONE, THE OLD FAMILIAR FASCES."

7/5/62

"SIR! WHAT ARE YOU DOING IN MY BOUDOIR?"

9/28/60

"WE HAVE A COMMON CULTURAL BACKGROUND."

2/26/64

"TRICKS OR TREATIES"
10/13/60

"GOOD HEAVENS–THAT STUFF IS DANGEROUS!"
12/21/60

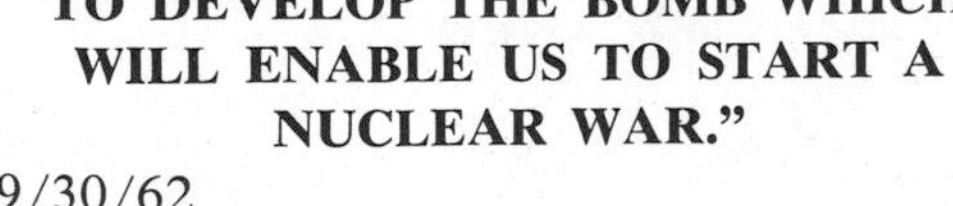
"BUT CHEER UP–WE HOPE SOON TO DEVELOP THE BOMB WHICH WILL ENABLE US TO START A NUCLEAR WAR."
9/30/62

"THE PROSPECTS FOR A TEST BAN ARE HOPEFUL..."
7/19/63

TEN YEARS IN KOREA
4/20/60

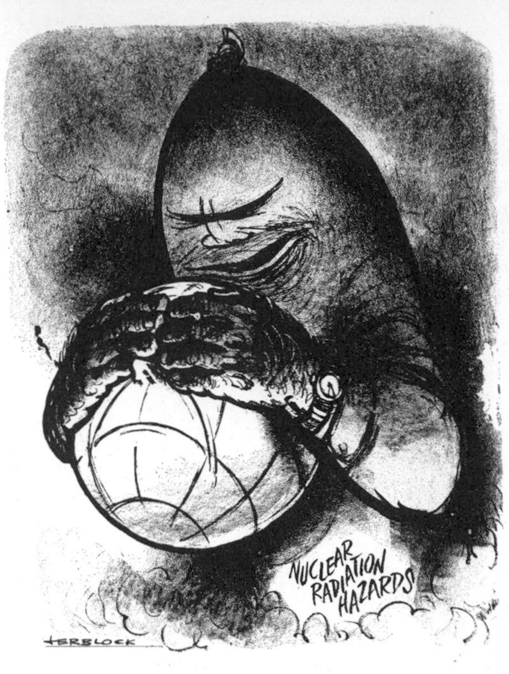

"GUESS WHO?"
9/16/62

A ROSE TO WEAR FOREVER
5/28/64

4. Frontier Town

WHEN Senator John F. Kennedy was running for President in 1960 and was asked on a TV interview program to fill in with a few words till a station break, he said that he had recently been initiated into an Indian tribe, and now when he watched the westerns, he found himself cheering for "our" guys.

There *is* always another side, and of course there must have been many a brave and squaw proud to see the youngster grow up into a redskin full-blooded American boy, going out for all the track, trail and warpath teams, and winning his scalp in the spear throw and tomahawk swing.

Happily, in the New Frontier town of Washington, Mr. Kennedy was on *our* side. And life on that frontier was never dull.

When this new sheriff moved in, the Redmen were already established in nearby Cuba, the beat of tom-toms could be heard from the

"SADDLE UP. WE CAN STILL HEAD 'EM OFF AT THE GULCH."

3/28/61

"NO FAIR—I CAN'T AFFORD A GUN."
8/11/59

Congo, war dances had been going on in Berlin, and not long before, Khru-Chief Ni-Ki-Ta had beaten his moccasin in the U.N. meeting house and let out the whoops of a man determined to behead the leadership there. In the Great Open Spacerace, the moon was already shining on his banner; and the sounds of Redman's shots were already coming from Laos and Viet-Nam, outposts at which some of "our guys" were already serving.

The Old General who had recently been in charge of the fort had shown a fondness for cannons, but hadn't made much provision for Indian-style fighting. And the Economy general store was looking somewhat rundown.

Some fellows loaded with Old Jim Crow were whooping it up at the Stars and Bars Saloon; the Birchbark boys were ready to go loco on red-eye; and the AMA tribe of political medicine men were scattering wampum around as they cried their own threatening chants at the new frontier.

Sheriff Kennedy's deputy, Newton Minow, was scouting the wastelands, while chief deputy Stewart Udall was busy keeping the guys from the badlands from grabbing the goodlands.

And all the time, skulking around in the background, was Big Atom, the roughest, toughest guy that ever lived.

One of the things that made life troublesome in Frontier Town was the Capitol Hill country boys, who didn't seem to be working as hard as they should have. Some of those boys just lazed around; others actually went in for hold-ups; and a few of the boys even tied up the public schoolmarm.

As far as the Capitol Hill crowd is concerned, Washington was actually a frontier city long before the New Frontier, permitting the maximum individuality, responsibility or irresponsibility, and generally characterized by self-protection. An old feature of this frontier has been occasional feuding with the man in the White House or with other Hill folk.

At home on the Hill are the brave, the strictly expedient, the loud, the quiet, and such an old-fashioned team of performers as Senate Minority Leader Everett Dirksen and House Minority Leader Charles Halleck. Their occasional press reports and televised statements came to be known as the Ev and Charlie Show, a tag that brought no end of calls to the TV editor from readers who wanted to know why

"IN TEN THOUSAND WORDS OR LESS, EV—IS IT TRUE YOU'RE VERBOSE?"

5/21/61

this "Ev and Charlie Show" was not listed among the weekly television programs.

As for law and order, a President does his best to maintain order and hopes to get his laws. But some of the Hill veterans are laws unto themselves.

I thought the President and Vice-President and their party leaders in Congress should have pushed for rules reforms at the very beginning —and especially after their victories in the Congressional elections of 1962.

A number of the cartoons were on the subject of Congressional delays and recalcitrance, and focused, as usual, on the things left undone. But as President Kennedy observed, you have to judge a Congress on its entire two-year span.

I recall a picture story in *Parade* about a visit of correspondent Fred Blumenthal to the President's country home, Glen Ora. When the two men emerged from the house, the President tried to interest his dog in chasing a stick, which he threw around and tossed back and forth with Mr. Blumenthal—while the dog looked on listlessly. Finally, Mr. Kennedy gave up his efforts to engage the dog in play, and as he and the correspondent walked on, he tossed the stick away. At that point the dog ran like crazy and tore back with the stick in his mouth, tail wagging, and grinning as broadly as a dog can grin.

It is sometimes that way with Congress, which, at the end of a term comes through with a whoosh—sometimes with good legislation and sometimes with a grabbag of all kinds of things.

I still think there's a great need for revising procedures in Washington and elsewhere. But that, as the saying goes, is another story.

However, if you're interested and aren't doing anything else at the moment, it just happens to be the next chapter. ■

"GENTLEMEN, THIS HERE TOWN IS DUE FOR SOME CHANGES."

5/11/61

"IT LOOKS LIKE THE SAME OLD TRIBE AT THE PASS."

1/29/61

GATEWAY TO THE NEW FRONTIER
11/17/60

"I THOUGHT *YOU* WERE BRINGING THE MATCHES."
4/7/63

"I GUESS YOU FELLOWS BETTER GO ON AHEAD."
8/20/63

"THEY WENT THATAWAY."

12/30/60

"WATER!"

2/24/61

"WE HAVE A FEW PRIMITIVE CONDITIONS HERE, TOO."

10/22/61

"NOW, HAS EVERYONE GOT ONE OF THESE LITTLE FIGURES AND A SET OF PINS?"

11/29/60

"I DON'T KNOW IF IT'S SOLID ENOUGH TO HOLD BOTH OF US."

1/4/62

"GEE, THAT WAS EXCITING— SOME DAY, LET'S ACTUALLY GO IN."

1/10/63

"WHO NEEDS IT? WE'RE STILL MOVING, AREN'T WE?"

8/9/63

"WE'VE BEEN KILLING 'EM IN WASHINGTON."

3/30/61

THE SLAPSTICK BOYS IN THE EMERGENCY ROOM
4/7/61

"IF THEY GO FOR THIS, HOW MUCH SHALL WE MAKE 'EM PAY NEXT TIME?"
6/25/61

"WE'RE NOT *THAT* ANXIOUS TO BALANCE THE BUDGET."
7/12/62

THE UNCERTAIN-TRUMPET SECTION
2/17/63

"TELL US WHAT SACRIFICES WE CAN MAKE! –INSTEAD OF THE ONES THAT ARE NEEDED, THAT IS."
5/31/61

"GOODNESS, ARE YOU THE BEAT AND ANGRY YOUNG MEN I'VE HEARD SO MUCH ABOUT?"
3/11/61

"YOU MEAN HELP AMERICANS TWICE IN ONE YEAR?"
9/27/63

"HOPE YOU DIDN'T TAKE ANYTHING PERSONALLY–THE FACT IS WE DON'T EVEN GET ALONG WITH EACH OTHER."
10/14/62

5. Self-Government for Americans!

THERE HAS BEEN much speculation about how newly emerging nations in Africa and elsewhere will fare with self-government. A more immediate question is: How have we been doing the last few decades on self-government in the United States? The answer is: Not so good. And the reason is that we haven't been getting the representative government that was designed for us.

This has come about because of (*a*) voting restrictions, (*b*) nonrepresentative apportionment systems, and (*c*) nonrepresentative procedures in Congress.

As for the voting, I can't recall an election year—or for that matter a year between elections—when there haven't been articles and editorials about our sacred right, even duty, to vote. The writers of these patriotic pieces weep for our country because so many Americans don't appreciate the precious heritage that our ancestors fought and bled and died for; and they tell us how lucky we are over here, and ask how it is that so many Americans just don't take the trouble to vote.

If they'll stop sniffling and listen, I can tell them. One reason millions of Americans haven't cast ballots on election days is that they haven't been allowed to. And I'm not referring only to Mississippi, Alabama and Virginia.

Carl Sandburg tells of the man who boasted

"YOU SEE—FIRST WOMEN, THEN NEGROES, NOW CONGRESSMEN AND SENATORS."
12/28/62

to a Ku Kluxer that he was not merely a 100 per cent American but a *200* per cent American, because he hated *everybody,* regardless of race, color or creed. Nondemocracy has not been that inclusive, but it has been broad enough so that it has not narrowly limited itself to one color or one geographic section. Disenfranchisement in some Southern states has been the most deliberate, the most flagrant and the most odious. But such racial discrimination, in itself, has not accounted for most of the involuntary non-voting in the U. S. And despite the remedies of the 1964 Civil Rights Act, millions will continue to be short on suffrage.

I'm one of them. As a resident of the District of Columbia, I haven't done much voting for the past fifteen years or so, since I lost my voting rights elsewhere. Neither have hundreds of thousands of other Washingtonians.

For years I used to render myself suspect with nervous groups by declaring that residents of the capital of the United States were permitted less democracy than the residents of the capital of Soviet Russia, where a sufficiently hardy soul could at least write in a name that was not on the approved list. In 1874, Congress withdrew suffrage from the District of Columbia and left D.C. residents with no vote at all. The passage of the 23rd Amendment allowed Washingtonians to vote for President and Vice-President of the United States beginning with the 1964 election—and not a moment too soon. Those are nice offices to vote for, but that is still the only balloting for public office allowed in a city with a larger population than any of ten states of the union—each of which has two senators, at least one congressman, a governor, mayors, councils, legislatures and the rest.

And for those who think District residents get some kind of special tax break, we don't. The Federal income tax, District income tax, sales taxes, and all other taxes are paid—but without any voice as to how much, or how they shall be collected, or how they shall be spent. There used to be an old saying about taxation without representation. The suggestion has been made that the case of the capital of the United States be brought before the U.N. like that of other colonial territories.

"IT'S INTERESTING TO SEE WHAT THEY'RE DOING IN THE UNITED STATES."

11/5/60

"ALOHA."

3/13/59

"NAH, YOU AIN'T GOT ENOUGH EDJICCASHUN TO VOTE."
12/10/58

THE STILL-FORGOTTEN MAN
8/18/61

ANIMAL FARM
4/2/61

Among others in the U.S. who "don't take the trouble to vote" are an estimated three million American migrant workers, who not only can't vote, but also miss out on minimum health and education standards for themselves and their families.

Millions of other Americans lose out on voting rights because they move from one house or apartment to another—sometimes from state to state, sometimes from one precinct or county to another. The suffrage of these people depends on the whimsical standards of various state and local regulations regarding residence and other voting requirements.

In 1963 a report on registration and voting participation was made by a President's Commission headed by Census Bureau Director Richard M. Scammon. It noted that some registration systems operate like obstacle courses for the voters, and that many states make absentee voting difficult or impossible. "Restrictive legal and administrative procedures..." it said, "disenfranchise millions."

The American Heritage Foundation made a study of the subject and listed a number of vote-deprived groups—including some 800,000 brides who temporarily lose the franchise during a year because their names have been changed by marriage (going under an alias, as it were, and maybe guilty of moving to a new home besides). This Foundation has estimated the number of American adults disqualified from voting at around 19,000,000.

Suppose only a fraction of that number were disqualified. Since the 1960 Presidential election was decided by less than 120,000 votes, and since many state elections were decided by only a few hundred votes or a few dozen, a matter of a few million could make the difference between victory or defeat, a close squeak or a landslide "mandate."

The second bulwark of misrepresentative government has been unfair apportionment, an inequity that the Supreme Court moved to correct in cases affecting legislative districts—and God bless this honorable court for holding that under the equal protection of the laws, one man's vote should count for as much as another's. In our more-than-70-per-cent urban nation, the city voter—if he has been able to

"YOU MEAN, SUH, LET THEM MINGLE BALLOTS IN THE SAME BOX WITH OURS?"

8/22/61

"I THINK THEM FEDS GOT ME, BOYS, BUT I KNOW YOU'LL CARRY ON."

8/28/62

vote—has often received what amounts to one-half or one-tenth of the vote of a man in a rural area. It will be some time before fair apportionment is achieved to provide something closer to equality in Congressional and state elections. But in one revealing case the effect came quickly.

Judge James C. Davis of the Fifth District of Georgia had served eight consecutive terms in the U.S. Congress, where, as a member of the District Committee, he operated as a self-appointed ruler over the subject people of Washington, D.C. He had even been placed in nomination, by the Georgia delegation to a Democratic convention, for his party's nomination for the Presidency of the United States. Well, one of the first effects of the court reapportionment decisions was the elimination of the county unit system in Georgia, through which rural districts heavily outweighed the more populous areas. In the election of the following year, James C. Davis was defeated. It turned out that this eight-term Congressman, this segregationist who held sway over 800,000 residents of the District of Columbia and had a voice in all American government, did not even represent the voters of his own Congressional district in Georgia.

As democracy is reinstituted throughout the country other faces will disappear in time from the state and from the national scene.

In Alabama, in 1962, Governor Wallace was elected with a total of 303,987 votes. But the Census Bureau lists the potential vote in Alabama as 1,848,000. It's sometimes said that we shouldn't indict a whole section of the country, and I agree. I don't know that Governor Wallace is the people's choice in Alabama, and we won't know until free elections are held there.

Senator James O. Eastland of Mississippi, in *his* last election, received 244,341 votes in a state where the U. S. Census Bureau gives the number of potential voters as 1,179,000. Whether this man, who holds tremendous power in the U. S. Senate, could win a free election in his state is also an unanswered question.

Let's face it—there are quite a few people in the United States who think that representative government is all right for the Fourth of July but not for the first Tuesday after the first Monday in November. And some farm area poli-

"DEALER WINS AND WINNER DEALS."
11/23/60

"YOU CAN'T SAY WE'RE DENYING YOUR RIGHT TO VOTE."
4/23/61

"WE'VE FLUNKED OUT IN MATH ALREADY."

5/6/62

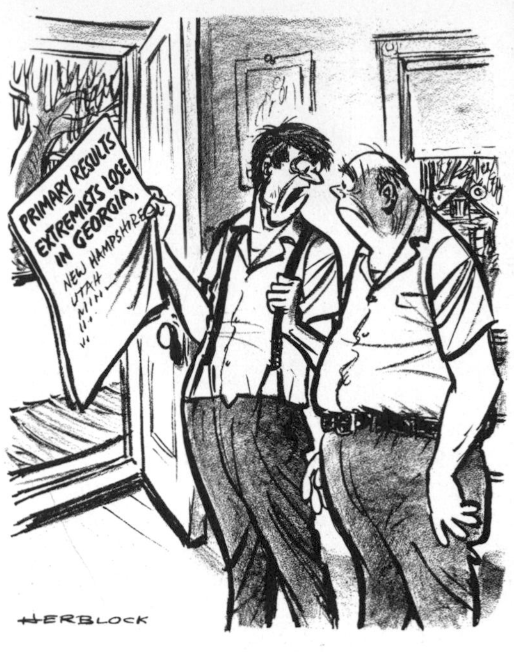

"WE DIDN'T GO FAR ENOUGH. WE SHOULD HAVE BEEN AGAINST VOTING BY WHITE PEOPLE TOO."

9/14/62

ticians have even been frank enough to assert that their sparsely populated areas *should* carry more weight than heavily populated urban centers.

There is, incidentally, a vague but still persistent idea that some special virtue attaches to rural areas, God's great outdoors and early rising, and that city folk—well, they live in wicked cities. And cities have wicked political machines. Around the turn of the century when municipal corruption was a big topic, they did indeed—and for some time later. But with the decline in illiteracy, and with such New Deal reforms as Social Security, there was a decline in the power to buy or influence votes with a scuttle of coal, a basket of food, a drink of whisky or a couple of dollars. The big city machines also declined, and few remain, or retain much of their old power.

The muckrakers of half a century ago wrote of The Shame of the Cities, but the shame of the cities today is largely the shame of state governments that shortchange the city dwellers on their votes and on returns for their tax dollars. As the population has shifted to great urban areas (which now even cross state lines), the greatest of vote frauds has been the built-in fraud of minority rural domination of states.

Even in terms of specific corruption, it's interesting to note that in the 1960 national election, when charges were made that the Illinois electoral vote had been "stolen" in Chicago, in Cook County, the demands for a recount of that urban vote suddenly died down when it was proposed that there be a recount of the *entire* state of Illinois, including the rural areas.

I think that for many years the most tightly controlled and ruthless political machine in the country has been the Byrd machine in Virginia. Its reign has been so all-embracing that in 1964 many Republican politicians in Virginia—including Byrd-oriented Congressman Broyhill, a nominal Republican—protested their party's even fielding a candidate against Senator Byrd.

And this brings us to the third, final, triple-riveted defense used by forces opposed to repre-

"THIS IS WHAT YOU MIGHT CALL DEFENSE IN DEPTH."
1/4/63

"IT WAS AMUSING TO SEE THOSE LIBERALS TRY TO HANG THINGS UP WITH A FILIBUSTER."
8/23/62

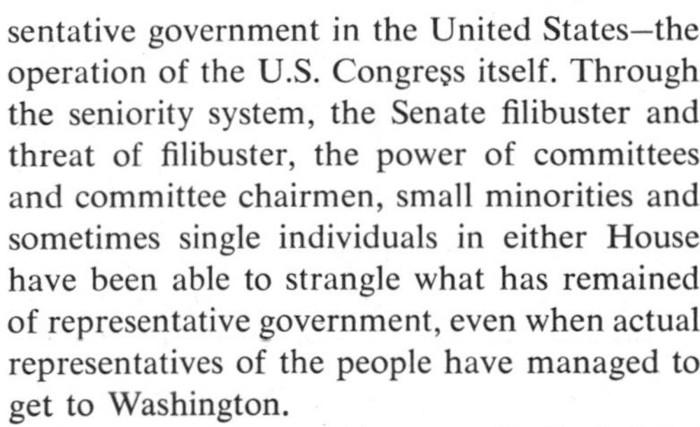

sentative government in the United States—the operation of the U.S. Congress itself. Through the seniority system, the Senate filibuster and threat of filibuster, the power of committees and committee chairmen, small minorities and sometimes single individuals in either House have been able to strangle what has remained of representative government, even when actual representatives of the people have managed to get to Washington.

One congressman, Wayne Aspinall of Colorado, kept the Wilderness Bill tied up for years. One congressman, Otto Passman of Louisiana, has for years managed to force cuts in all foreign aid bills, and screamed bloody murder when President Johnson outmaneuvered him on the 1964 bill. One congressman, Howard Smith, of the House Rules Committee, has often been able to bottle up any legislation he chose simply by taking off for his farm and literally closing the door to action.

When the seniority system, which gives such men their power, comes up for discussion, some congressman who has been around long enough to develop a taste for good vintage authority will ask what better system could replace it. This is an old method of shifting the discussion to some other proposal, which is pretty sure to contain some imperfection that can be pounced upon. The best answer to that question came at a dinner one evening when a noncongressional government official was asked by a congressman, "Ah, but can you suggest a better system?"

"Why, yes," came the instant reply. "You could cut cards; you could roll dice; you could turn a roulette wheel; you could draw straws; you could flip coins; you could spin a bottle..." The congressman with the long-time seniority found himself something of a first-time mute.

Some argument might be made for the seniority system if the men who gained most of the seniority were not so often those from districts or states where there has been the least voting, and where democracy and the free exchange of ideas—and politicians—have been least likely to prevail.

Here is a list of states in which the lowest percentage of persons of voting age cast ballots —all of these states well below the 50 per cent mark. Reading from near-bottom to bottom, they are:

Louisiana
Texas
Arkansas
Virginia
Alabama
Georgia
South Carolina
Mississippi

Now, from the Congressional Directory of 1964, here are some of the men who, through their committee positions, exercise control over the U.S. Congress. These are in each case the chairman and top seniority members of the majority party. This, however, is no recommendation for their Republican counterparts, about whom much else could be written.

The top ranking Majority members on 10 of the 16 standing committees of the Senate are:

AGRICULTURE AND FORESTRY
Allen J. Ellender, of Louisiana *(chairman)*
Olin D. Johnston, of South Carolina

APPROPRIATIONS *(Meets upon call of chairman)*
Carl Hayden, of Arizona *(chairman)*
Richard B. Russell, of Georgia
Allen J. Ellender, of Louisiana
Lister Hill, of Alabama
John L. McClellan, of Arkansas
A. Willis Robertson, of Virginia

ARMED SERVICES
Richard B. Russell, of Georgia *(chairman)*
John Stennis, of Mississippi
Harry Flood Byrd, of Virginia

BANKING AND CURRENCY
A. Willis Robertson, of Virginia *(chairman)*
John J. Sparkman, of Alabama

FINANCE
Harry Flood Byrd, of Virginia *(chairman)*
Russell B. Long, of Louisiana

FOREIGN RELATIONS
J. W. Fulbright, of Arkansas *(chairman)*
John J. Sparkman, of Alabama

GOVERNMENT OPERATIONS
John L. McClellan, of Arkansas *(chairman)*

JUDICIARY
James O. Eastland, of Mississippi *(chairman)*
Olin D. Johnston, of South Carolina
John L. McClellan, of Arkansas

LABOR AND PUBLIC WELFARE
Lister Hill, of Alabama *(chairman)*

POST OFFICE AND CIVIL SERVICE
Olin D. Johnston, of South Carolina *(chairman)*

The top ranking Majority members of more than half of the standing committees of the House are:

AGRICULTURE
Harold D. Cooley, of North Carolina *(chairman)*
W. R. Poage, of Texas
George M. Grant, of Alabama
E. C. Gathings, of Arkansas
John L. McMillan, of South Carolina
Thomas G. Abernethy, of Mississippi
Watkins M. Abbitt, of Virginia

APPROPRIATIONS *(Meets upon call of chairman)*
George H. Mahon, of Texas *(chairman)*

ARMED SERVICES
Carl Vinson, of Georgia *(chairman)*
L. Mendel Rivers, of South Carolina

BANKING AND CURRENCY
Wright Patman, of Texas *(chairman)*
Albert Rains, of Alabama

DISTRICT OF COLUMBIA
John L. McMillan, of South Carolina *(chairman)*
Thomas G. Abernethy, of Mississippi
Howard W. Smith, of Virginia

HOUSE ADMINISTRATION
Omar Burleson, of Texas *(chairman)*

INTERSTATE AND FOREIGN COMMERCE
Oren Harris, of Arkansas *(chairman)*
John Bell Williams, of Mississippi
Kenneth A. Roberts, of Alabama

RULES *(Meets upon call of chairman)*
Howard W. Smith, of Virginia *(chairman)*
William M. Colmer, of Mississippi

UN-AMERICAN ACTIVITIES
Edwin E. Willis, of Louisiana *(chairman)*
William M. Tuck, of Virginia
Joe R. Pool, of Texas

VETERANS' AFFAIRS *(Meets upon call of chairman)*
Olin E. Teague, of Texas *(chairman)*
W. J. Bryan Dorn, of South Carolina

WAYS AND MEANS *(Meets upon call of chairman)*
Wilbur D. Mills, of Arkansas *(chairman)*

A number of these committee chairmen, who exercise a veto power never contemplated in the Constitution, will be recognized as those who decry "usurpation of power" by the President and by the Supreme Court.

Thanks to the Supreme Court's decisions on reapportionment and voting rights, and to the Civil Rights Act pushed by Presidents Kennedy and Johnson, representative government has been given a new lease on life in our country.

It's often said that we get the kind of government we deserve; but we *haven't* been getting the kind of government we deserve.

We won't get it till all Americans have equal voting rights and equal representation in state legislatures and in Congress—and in a Congress that can act. For this, rules reforms are still needed. At a minimum, they should include reform of the House Rules Committee to keep it from bottling up legislation, and alteration of the Senate filibuster rule to permit majority-rule voting after a reasonable period of debate.

It can be said that the 88th Congress put on a good finish, passing the tax bill, the civil rights bill, and other measures in its second session. Much of this must be attributed to the patient preliminary work of President Kennedy, much to the long, strong arm and special skill of President Johnson, who has a way with congressmen.

But there's no reason why a Congress, really representing the people and in Washington to get work done, should not have taken up the whole Kennedy program while he was President. There's no reason why the civil rights bill should have been delayed through a 75-day filibuster and all the pre-filibuster threats and delays; there's no reason why it should take wheedling, *quid pro quos,* special White House magic, or anything but the wishes of senators and representatives themselves to get bills out on the floor where they can vote on them.

In each House of Congress the rules can be revised, as they have been in the past, at the beginning of any two-year session. Congressional reform can be made a prime campaign issue any time civic-minded groups will work to make it so. There's no reason why candidates for the Senate and the House, who are questioned about their attitudes on de Gaulle, Viet-Nam and Zanzibar, shouldn't be questioned on how they stand on putting their own houses in order.

Those who do have the vote can use it to make congressmen make Congress an effective and representative body. And this, in turn, will release measures like the District of Columbia Home Rule bill, which Congress would long ago have passed if the bill could have been pried out of a committee. Government by and for the people sounds so good that I think we should get it. ■

"WHAT DOES HE THINK THIS IS —A LEGISLATIVE BODY?"

2/21/63

2/26/60

"LET 'EM VOTE FOR CONGRESSMEN –LONG AS WE CAN KEEP THE CONGRESSMEN FROM VOTING FOR THEM."

12/19/62

"YOU'RE OUT OF ORDER."

1/8/63

"THUMBS OFF!"

6/18/64

"OUR POSITION HAS BEEN MISREPRESENTED. WE ONLY WANT TO DENY THE U.S. SENATE THE RIGHT TO VOTE."
3/3/60

"WHAT'S THIS UGLY TALK ABOUT APPLYING RULES TO ME?"
12/7/60

"IT'S A PLEASURE TO WORK AT YOUR SIDE–CAN YOU MOVE OVER A BIT MORE?"
11/22/62

"THERE'S SOME DANGEROUS RADICAL TALK ABOUT DEMOCRACY GOING AROUND AGAIN."

12/27/60

HEAR YE! HEAR YE!

3/27/62

"HO HUM–IT'S SURE DULL AROUND HERE."

8/8/62

COLD WAR AT HOME

11/6/63

"THERE ARE SOME SURPLUSES I DON'T MIND."

12/14/60

"AS YOUR REPRESENTATIVE, I PROMISE TO CONTINUE OUR FIGHT AGAINST REDISTRICTING."

8/11/61

"IF YOU DON'T LIKE THIS SITUATION, YOU CAN CAST YOUR TWENTIETH OF A VOTE AGAINST IT."

10/13/61

"HMPH—THERE'S NOTHING IN THOSE SILOS BUT PEOPLE."

2/22/62

6. Goldwaterland

ONE OF the greatest amusement centers in the world is "The Magic Kingdom"—Disneyland. Millions of people have spent delightful hours and days there, and Mr. Khrushchev was reported to be disappointed when security reasons prevented him from making a short-notice visit to it when he was in this country.

It was inevitable that there would be imitations of this charming place, with variations of its Main Street, Adventureland, Frontierland, Fantasyland and Tomorrowland attractions. But by far the most ambitious and successful of these is:

THE MAGIC REPUBLIC
(not a democracy)
GOLDWATERLAND

This place Mr. Khrushchev could not visit even with advance notice.

Here, as in Disneyland, you enter via Main Street, and immediately you are back to the turn of the century. Here are old-fashioned stores and buildings and shady trees—everything delightful and good and nostalgic.

Your host, the proprietor, smiles as he shows you around and points out his old family department store. He kids about being old-fashioned himself, and chuckles because he knows that we all have a longing for the old days as we like to think they were. It's all so restful and easy and charming: the old soda parlor, the old trolley, the old drugstore—but with modern miracle drugs and indoor plumbing—everything with the best of yesterday and today. And everything so cheap . . . just pennies and nickels really. Today's salaries in our pockets and all those things in the shops at the prices of the Gay Nineties. And taxes, hah! Not much government or anything like that to worry about. Everybody well fed, nobody ever ill, everything spic-and-span. Not even any flies around the open grocery barrels in those dear old days before the bad days when "increasingly the Federal government sets standards of education, health and safety."

This is Never-Was Land.

IT DOESN'T EXIST and never did exist. But it is a tribute to the proprietor's ingenuity that he has been able to conjure it up and make it seem a place that actually was and to which we could really return. It is the perfect way to enter his world of fantasy, and he is aware of it.

While you are looking longingly at the stores with those wonderfully low prices in the windows, your host firmly steers you into the next section—Frontierland. *Old* Frontierland, that is.

You ride the old Santa Fe train through Arizona, which produces a rugged, outdoor, All-American American. Here is frontier life in comfort, and without any uncertainties. And then there's the delightful steamboat ride down the Mississippi—and there's Mississippi itself! And Alabama too! And the old plantation and the cotton, and the darkies laughing and singing. Everybody happy with his state in life and his state's rights. It's charming, and it looks almost real.

AND NOW further down the river is Adventureland, with its own boat ride through the thick jungle. Adventure is on every side and around every turn in the winding river. A rhinoceros suddenly appears beside the boat and your host shoots him. A crocodile opens its jaws and snaps them shut just short of the boat. Your host shoots him. A gigantic yellow snake-like Chinese dragon hisses as it drops from an overhanging tree. Your host shoots him. A huge Russian bear lunges toward the boat as it rounds a bend. Your host has only to frown and the bear backs away apologetically; your host makes a motion to reach for his gun and the bear turns tail and runs.

It is such fun. All the surprises and thrills of adventure and no danger at all! You marvel at the ingenious machinery that draws the boat along its underwater cable, that produces the hisses, the near misses, and the growls and retreats of those mechanical animals. And maybe you wonder for just a moment how you and your intrepid captain would fare if this were a real boat in a real river and those were real animals. But by now you have come to Fantasyland.

HERE ARE all kinds of identified flying objects—including Peter Pan, whose spirit really fills the whole of Goldwaterland. We seem to fly, too, as countryside and villages appear to pass beneath us.

What remarkable effects the proprietor of this park has created! He gives you the feeling of pushing boldly forward while actually retreating from reality.

Instead of seeing enchanted castles and thatched huts below, as in Disneyland, you pass over entire individual states—each one separated from the others by a wide gulf—and all separated by an even wider gulf from the eastern seaboard, which is crumbling into the ocean. They are walled off completely from Washington, D. C., which is falling into decay. As you soar above each separate, sovereign state, you can look right down into the little streets with no crime on them; and into the little houses where everyone is well fed and content; and the little shops where everyone has a job—and all because the wicked witches of Washington, D. C., are dead. Fantasyland is so dreamy that you can't be sure whether you've wakened suddenly or have gone right on dreaming as you drift into Tomorrowland.

Here the proprietor is bursting with vigor, and apparently this is the part toward which he has been anxious to hurry you all along. You step into his very own jet plane which nearly collides with another plane while he is explaining that nowhere in the United States Constitution is the Federal government given specific authority to regulate airplane flights, and that never in the Constitutional Convention was this even discussed.

By the time he has finished expounding on this, you leave the jet and the host takes you on his Mental Monorail that speeds toward a mountain higher than Disney's Matterhorn. This is the No-Matterhorn. And you transfer again to make the final stage to the top in a missile-shaped vehicle. With a great thrust you are off on the FuNuclear railway, and soon emerge at the mountain peak.

HERE at the very top is something that looks like a combination IBM machine and ham radio outfit, with several banks of flashing buttons. Your host presses one and some cards pop out containing various conflicting statements on issues. "Wrong button," he says with a laugh, and presses another. Nothing happens. He puts on his spectacles, from which the lenses have been removed, and peers closely at the button. "No wonder!" He laughs again. "That launched a missile to New Hampshire. I must have goofed somewhere. Let's see now." He presses a couple more buttons, one of which produces birch beer, and finally hits one that releases a box containing a non-survival kit that includes a Superman belt, an American flag, and a small tactical nuclear bomb. As you buckle on the belt, he drapes the flag over your shoulders like a Superman cape, places the bomb in your arms, points toward the horizon and says, "Eastward lies the enemy."

"Where?" you ask.

"Practically anywhere eastward," he replies, "Moscow, Washington, New York, Pennsylvania, Walter Reuther's office in Detroit . . . wait a minute." He goes back and examines the buttons again. "I'm not sure, but I think I pressed the ultimatum button for Moscow. But it may have been the one to Washington." As he takes your arm and leads you to the brink, he says, "Maybe you can tell as you fly over."

"Fly? In this?"

He whips off his glasses and looks stern. "You don't like the flag? You don't believe in it? It has always flown proudly," he says.

"But not with me in it."

He looks still more stern. *"A craven fear of death is entering the American consciousness*—that's from one of my books. And *we must think of the whole man.* They keep putting that in all my writings."

"I was just thinking of the whole man," you murmur.

WHILE YOU HAVE BEEN talking, he has grasped your arm and moved you to the very edge of the abyss. "Remember," he says, quoting himself or his writers again, "we must always try to engage the enemy at times and places and with weapons of our own choosing."

"Wait!" you cry; but there is no echo—not in this place.

Instead, there is, of course, a choice. And as you look down the steep precipice and feel the steady pressure on your back, you realize what it is.

If you have any conservative conscience at all, you'll Take The Initiative and go The Voluntary Way. ■

"AS I WAS SAYING, A TEST-BAN AGREEMENT MIGHT HAVE RESULTED IN A FATAL GAP."

8/14/63

"WHO WOULD HAVE THOUGHT THAT THE REVOLUTION CONTAINED SO MANY TRAITORS?"

4/12/60

7. Cuba, From Beard to Razor's Edge

THIS IS a short Cuban overflight in cartoons, beginning with the exciting news of the overthrow of the Batista dictatorship that brought in a bearded New Year boy on January 1, 1959 —and stopping just short of the nerve-wracking missile crisis of 1962, when the world might have gone *Bang* like a loaded cigar.

The gambling cartoon appeared eight days after Castro took over, and caused some surprise because it ran while enthusiasm for the new regime was still high. I can't claim prescience about all that followed; and in fact I still had hopes for a better deal for Cuba. It was

"THE REBEL CLAIMS ARE GREATLY EXAGGERATED, AND THAT SHOOTING YOU HEAR IS JUST STATIC."

12/30/58

"GAMBLING ISN'T BEING ENTIRELY ELIMINATED."

1/9/59

"WE MAY HAVE SOME DOUBLE-HEADERS."

1/25/59

"TOMORROW MORNING, SUNNY– PRAISE FIDEL–WITH RAIN IN AFTERNOON–DAMN THOSE AMERICANS–"

3/13/60

drawn on a simple day-to-day call'-em-the-way-they-look basis, when Castro began by closing the gambling spots, showing a zest for executions, and postponing the hope of early elections that he had previously promised.

The reader will not find in this little text a hot news flash that there was a fiasco at the Bay of Pigs,. a scene which has undergone political beachcombing for some years now. The failure there was so quick, so obvious, and so completely acknowledged that it hardly required a detective–or a CIA man–to notice that something had gone amiss. I would like to get in a few words, though, about the release-of-prisoners issue that followed. This was a hot one at the time, though not so well remembered now.

The original proposal was for the release of prisoners in exchange for tractors–although Castro shifted on the matter of what kind of machinery he had in mind; and it turned out that he wanted something considerably more than agricultural machines.

But the issue here was whether a group of Americans–pretty obviously abetted by the U.S. government–should engage in such a swap at all. There were loud cries of "Ransom!" "Millions for defense but not one cent for tribute!" And the famous ultimatum dispatched by Theodore Roosevelt and John Hay, "... Perdicaris alive, or Raisuli dead," was tossed about to suggest that any deal on behalf of the prisoners represented a craven submission and a betrayal of our national honor. In an article appearing over his name in the *Saturday Evening Post,* Senator Barry Goldwater said, "Of course the left wing in American politics sparked the ridiculous and ill-fated effort to submit to Castro's prisoner-tractor deal."

Those who raised the hullabaloo made no distinction, however, between the circumstances of Americans being snatched up and carried off to be held for a price–and counterrevolution-

"DON'T PUSH—THERE'S PLENTY FOR ALL OF YOU."
5/4/61

"DON'T THINK I'M TRYING TO WEASEL OUT OR ANYTHING."
6/9/61

ists who had been captured by the government they sought (with our planning) to overthrow. From the cries that were raised, you might have supposed that Cuban pirates had landed at Miami Beach and dashed back to the ship and to Cuba with All-American bathing girls over their shoulders.

Any government, however much we dislike it, can be expected to defend itself against invasion or attempted overthrow, and not only to take prisoners but to execute them. Since the men captured at the Bay had acted under American direction—and very bad direction—it seemed to me we had an obligation to do whatever we reasonably could to save them and to secure their release.

If our national honor was involved, it was in just the opposite way from that depicted by the people who screamed "Ransom!" And even from the most pragmatic viewpoint, if we were ever again to abet or direct people in any such operation, the precedent of forsaking these men and leaving them to die or to rot in jails would hardly be an encouraging one.

Castro's weaseling on the tractor deal, and his changing terms through the long negotiations, at least served one good purpose: during all that time, the hysteria about ransom died down.

Mayor Fiorello LaGuardia once endeared himself to his constituents by saying, "When I pull a boner, it's a beaut!" In words less colorful but equally plain, President Kennedy took upon himself full responsibility for the disastrous invasion attempt, which had been conceived in the preceding administration. And in the quasi-official prisoner negotiations, he acted, as might have been expected, with honor, and with a responsibility all the more notable because he must certainly have known that the released men would not be uncritical of the government that had been to blame for the debacle in which they were captured. ■

"WHAT HAPPENS WHEN THEY RUN OUT OF FOREIGNERS?"
10/20/60

"WE MUST ELIMINATE FOREIGN INFLUENCES, SUCH AS VOTING BY CUBANS."
5/3/61

"ANOTHER HISTORIC FIRST!"
9/12/62

BEACHCOMBER
3/10/63

8. War and Peace

IN THE letters-to-the-editor columns I keep seeing communications signed "So-and-so, Col. U.S.A. retired," which talk lightly of tossing bombs around. And I wonder how many military men there may be in the not-yet-retired category who might also be characters out of *Dr. Strangelove*. It would be comforting to think that the urge to warlike statements or total destruction comes only with retirement, with not having enough to do to keep busy—and possibly represents only boredom with puttering about the back yard.

However, memories of General Edwin Walker on duty in Europe, of high officers indoctrinating the men in their commands with "Blue book" material akin to Mr. Robert Welch's, and of wild Blue-book-yonder Air Force manuals of a few years back do not give me the feeling that all the bomb enthusiasts are in retirement. And they don't induce peaceful sleep when *I* retire evenings.

I wonder if some of these officers, once they start up the ladder of authority, shouldn't come in for periodic checkups of some kind, just in order to make sure they're not suffering from non-combat fatigue.

And that goes for the reserve generals too—even more so when they get so fascinated with the jargon, the inside dope, and "the game" that they refer to defoliating trees with nuclear bombs, as if these were just larger versions of aerosol bombs or garden sprays.

"TO ARMS! THE SACK COATS ARE COMING."
11/20/63

ARMY EDUCATION PROGRAM
6/13/61

"HE DOES SEEM TO BE OUT OF UNIFORM—OR SOMETHING."
7/26/61

"OH, THE ARMY ISN'T SPONSORING —IT'S JUST *ASSISTING*."
9/29/61

TICK—TOCK—TICK
10/28/62

I can say of such generals what a famous general said of his troops: *Gad, sir, they may not frighten the enemy but they certainly frighten me.*

I think not only that "war is too important to be left to the generals," but that both war and peace are too important to be left to generals or pacifists—either or both. By pacifists I mean those people who think that the way to keep peace is to proclaim that our nation will never fight under any circumstances. If our country seriously adopted such a policy, it would be awfully hard for even a responsible leader of a "potential enemy" power to resist pressure from his own warhawks to move in—especially if he had a Chinese dragon breathing down his neck.

Those of us who lived through the post-World-War-I and pre-World-War-II decades of disillusionment learned that, as far as peace is concerned, all the desire in the world—our part of the world—was not enough to prevent war; and that the theme for peace is not "Wishing Will Make It So." But such pacifists are a small minority and without any influence in government or in either major party.

The danger today is from those jingoistic military-minded politicos whose idea of a fine patriotic display is to demand louder threats and greater shows of force here, there and everywhere in the world.

President Kennedy's restraint, judgment and cool nerve in the 1962 Cuban missile crisis can serve as a history-book model of how the head of a great nation should act under severe pressure. When he proclaimed the blockade of Cuba and called for the removal of the missiles, he said that "... launching of a nuclear missile

THE OTHER ROAD

10/24/62

VOTE FOR ONE

10/23/62

from Cuba anywhere in this hemisphere will be regarded by us as an attack by the Soviet Union upon the United States . . ." But in the same speech he also spoke again of the desire for peace and for negotiation, and of the horrors of a nuclear war which no one could win. And he kept pressing for nuclear control.

The President's actions were effective because it was unmistakably clear that he was acting with reluctance but firm resolve in response to a most serious threat. And when he indicated that he was ready to pull the trigger, if necessary, it was obvious that he had thought carefully and that he meant it.

It might be asked if this was not "brinkmanship"—a policy which had been the subject of much criticism in the past—and the answer is: Definitely not.

As I've understood and used that term, it is not just by alliteration related to bluff, bluster, brag, and backdown. To go "to the brink" or to threaten "massive retaliation" without meaning it—or to bluff and then brag about it—is to invite another country next time to go a little closer to the brink itself, and to increase the likelihood of both countries falling in.

President Kennedy did not rub in his triumph and he did not issue ultimatums—as some congressmen urged—for Russia to get all its men out of Cuba *pronto*.

Wise statesmen follow a kind of open-door policy. They allow an opponent to bow out gracefully rather than cornering him and leaving him no choice but to fight.

The pitcher that President Kennedy took to the deep dark well of nuclear destruction is one that cannot be taken there often. We hope it will never have to be taken to that well again.

"LET'S GET A LOCK FOR THIS THING."

11/1/62

But smaller men, heady with a victory not their own, have urged that we blockade Cuba again; threaten Russia with war; tell them to do as we say—or else; make them back down here and there, again—and again.

To engage in brinkmanship is foolhardy. For a man in high office to brag that he has practiced brinkmanship is to court unnecessary danger. But when a reserve-general politician *announces in advance* that brinkmanship is his plan—that fellow should turn in his flight jacket for a strait jacket.

If the head of a "potential enemy" nation would have a hard time resisting the pressure to move in on a country that proclaimed itself unwilling ever to fight, he would have an even harder time staying in power if he continually backed down in the face of threats. Even such nonbelligerent and unprepared governments as those of Neville Chamberlain and Jawaharlal Nehru fought back, under sufficient provocation.

There suddenly pops into mind the "Peanuts" strip in which Lucy points and shouts, to no one visible, "You! Do this. Hop to it! You there —do that! Hop to it! Do this. Do that! Hop to it!" The strip concludes with Linus saying, "You're right, Lucy—you'd make a good queen." We are not the queen; neither is Russia; neither is any other country. That kind of international off-with-their-heads queen exists only in Alice's Wonderland and in the minds of characters who belong there with her.

After the Cuban missile crisis, when the entire world was breathing a relieved sigh, a few trigger-happy politicians seemed rather unhappy about the lack of action. In an Associated Press article, James Marlow wrote about the plane hijacking incidents in which three or four U.S. planes were landed in Cuba, and 24 of Castro's planes were landed in the U.S.:

> The last of the hijacked American planes landed in Cuba was an airliner with 81 persons aboard. Castro returned the plane and the passengers.
>
> But before they knew what he was going to do, Senators Strom Thurmond (D-S.C.) and Barry Goldwater (R.-Ariz.) wanted Mr. Kennedy to order the plane returned within 24 hours or, although Castro had nothing to do with the hijacking, send U.S. forces into Cuba. Mr. Kennedy stayed calm. There have been no more hijackings.

"UH HUH...LISTEN...YEAH, TOO BAD...LISTEN...LET ME TELL YOU WHAT HAPPENED TO ME, KRISHNA...."
11/2/62

There was no war over Cuba either. But shortly after the Cuban crisis, war did break out in another part of the world. China invaded India, which, under the policies of Defense Minister Krishna Menon, was unprepared for the attack. Time moves rapidly, so perhaps it is best to explain that this is the "Krishna" to whom the bearded one is talking in the Fidel-on-the-phone cartoon. Also, shortly afterward, Mr. Menon left office.

Meanwhile, back at El Rancho in the Americas—a little more than two years after Dominican dictator Trujillo was killed and his family driven out of the Dominican Republic, and only nine months after the first elected government in 38 years took office, a military coup ousted the elected President, Juan Bosch. A few days later the President of Honduras was also forced out in a military coup.

But people who never tired of berating President Kennedy for the Bay of Pigs fiasco, and who constantly clamored for embargoes, blockades and troops, were remarkably cool about the loss of two elected, democratic governments within eight days. The ousted governments were working for reforms; and apparently it was the very fact that they were democratic and elected and for reform that made them suspect with the people here who keep hoping for a return to banana-republic days.

At the time of the Bay of Pigs invasion attempt, I recall listening to an oil company's unsunny radio commentators warn that when Castro was thrown out, his reforms must be rooted out too. Back to the old OLD days! And I remember thinking what great listening this must be for Cubans, if there was a chance for a popular uprising.

Now, with the removal of President Bosch, here were the same three-star unspecial oil spielers announcing over the radio that the ousting of President Bosch was in accordance with the will of the people, because he had become unpopular with them. This showed real clairvoyance on their part, since the Dominican Republic President-eject had been elected just nine months before—the only time in nearly four decades that the people of that unhappy country had a chance to express their choice.

LATIN-AMERICAN SHOWCASE
10/1/63

I thought our government might have done more at that time. I've always thought that free, democratic governments are entitled to the support of other free, democratic governments. And I think there is considerable difference between sending forces to overthrow a democratic government and sending forces to aid one that is fighting for its life.

But one of the difficulties in such situations is that the existing Latin governments are just as reluctant to call for U.S. help as we are reluctant to seem to be "intervening." And so, when the calls come, they come late.

About these Latin situations President Kennedy said, in answer to a news conference question, that we were doing the best we could. And I could sympathize with his predicament. At any rate, he didn't have to worry about stirring calls to action from Colonels, U.S.A., retired; or about warlike speeches by U.S. Senator-Generals. These fellows don't get too excited about preserving democracies—especially elected reform governments.

Land reform, higher income for the natives, all that stuff—probably socialistic or something—and next thing you know, they might even want to develop their own resources. The fact that anti-democratic, anti-reform military rule provides fertile ground for more Castroism is something to think about another time. No—for these people, it's nothing to think about at all, because it does not fit in with their devil theory of Communism.

The Goldwater word on the Dominican Republic situation came in a speech to an association of men who had served as wartime officers, most of them now retired or in reserve service. He not only applauded the military junta that otherthrew the democratic government but attacked the Kennedy Administration for not giving prompt recognition and support to the military gang.

The little men who have busy days tossing around explosive comments should not be in a position to do the same thing with bombs. For my part, I think more of them should follow the example of the sleepy boy in the tire ad and get ready to blow out their candles. It's time for them to rest their tired little down-filled heads, and *really* retire. ■

"I SAY WE'VE BEEN FOLLOWING A NO-WIN APPEASEMENT POLICY, COMRADES, AND I ASK, WHO LOST CHINA?"

11/6/62

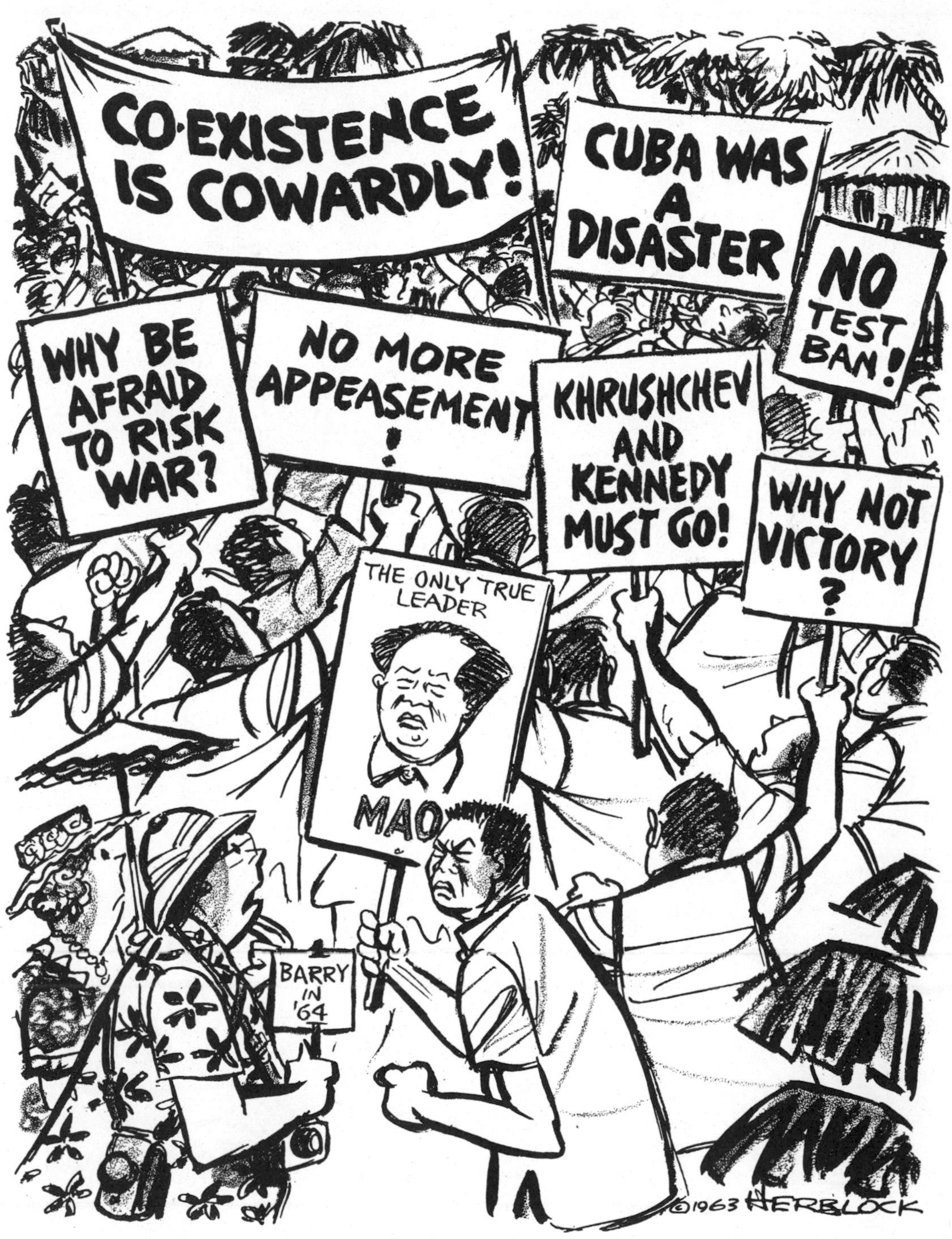

"OH, SORRY–WE THOUGHT IT WAS A GOLDWATER RALLY."

7/16/63

5/29/60

"OBSERVE CLOSELY, MI AMIGO—"
10/2/63

4/2/64

**"AND REMEMBER,
I'M GUARANTEED FOR LIFE.
NO OTHER DOCTOR-PRESIDENT
CAN MAKE THAT CLAIM!"**
4/3/64

"—AND BESIDES, IT'S ALL CHEAP RUSSIAN MERCHANDISE."
11/21/62

"WELL, TO START WITH, OF COURSE YOU KNOW HE'S A NUT."
11/27/62

"MAYBE I SHOULD TRY TO CUT DOWN."
2/8/63

"SO NICE YOU'RE GOING TO MOSCOW. PERHAPS THEY'LL LET YOU HAVE ANOTHER LOOK AT THOSE MISSILES."
4/19/63

"WHO SAID ANYTHING ABOUT DRIVING OUT CASTRO? WE'RE TALKING ABOUT KENNEDY."

2/26/63

"ABSOLUTELY! WE SHOULD STAY OUT OF FOREIGN AFFAIRS AND WE SHOULD MAKE OTHER COUNTRIES DO AS WE SAY."

2/25/64

"THINK IT'S COOLED OFF ENOUGH FOR US TO GO IN?"

3/11/64

"PRECISELY, GENERAL. IN THIS SPACE AGE, IT'S NOT ENOUGH TO BE ABLE TO DESTROY ONLY ONE PLANET."

4/15/64

9. Consumer's Guide to Washington

THERE ARE bewildering variations and brands of consumer items—not to mention some rather bewildering labels, like the one on a rug reading "genuine virgin nylon." But with some guidance the purchaser can cut down a little on the confusion about the relative merits and serviceability of these products. The public serviceability of public servants and public agencies is often more difficult for the consumer to determine.

I recall speaking with some college students some time in the nineteen-fifties, when one of the group told me of his failure to understand that day's cartoon, which concerned government regulatory agencies. This was not too surprising, since the agencies were doing so little regulating that many people didn't know they existed.

However, there were some changes in 1961. When Newton Minow became Chairman of the Federal Communications Commission, people learned that not only could they examine the quality of TV sets, but that there was an agency which could do something about the quality of the programs they received on those sets. And the FCC did something about the

RATING SERVICE
BROADCASTING INDUSTRY
ITEM: HEARINGS ON PROGRAM RATINGS DISCLOSE THAT ONE SAMPLED RADIO WAS ALWAYS KEPT ON TO AMUSE THE DOG WHEN NOBODY WAS HOME.
©HERBLOCK

HIS MASTER'S VOICE

4/5/63

receiving sets as well. It pushed legislation requiring that TVs include UHF reception.

In July 1964, Mr. Minow's successor, E. William Henry, specifically checkrated the members of the commission who were checkmating regulation, and cited a majority of four, who, he said, didn't care about the amount of advertising in radio and television and refused "even to grapple with" the problem of over-commercialization.

The airing of matters like that is even more interesting than the airing of the average broadcast.

A Congressional committee also aired the methods employed in establishing TV program "ratings" which proved to be both airy and eerie. Television critic Lawrence Laurent summed up the whole case of the networks and the "ratings" they live by with the classic story of a man who lost his pay each week playing roulette. When a friend said, "You dope—that wheel is fixed!" he replied, "I know, but it's the only roulette wheel in town."

Incidentally, the reliance of broadcasters on the rating services, and the FCC-majority deafness to too-loud and too-frequent commercials may help to explain the tremendous increase in the popularity of record-players in recent years.

"LET'S HAVE *MORE* *BIGGER-THAN-EVER* GOLDEN EGGS!"

11/10/61

"I SURRENDER, DEAR."

1/19/64

"HEADACHE? UPSET STOMACH? RINGING EARDRUMS? HERE'S REMARKABLE THREE-WAY NO-RELIEF!"

3/5/64

"YOU JUST DON'T SEEM TO FIT IN HERE."

4/29/60

Besides the FCC, another group that has been a special target of special interests is the Federal Power Commission, which has been under heavy attack by the natural gas producers. They claimed that the FPC was incapable of regulating gas prices, but felt they were perfectly capable of regulating the FPC—where the balance of power and the public interest has also rested on a majority of one. The natural gas producers have been aided in their efforts by highly paid public relations organizations, and by a number of supposed public servants in Congress. Some of these seem to be under the impression that the agencies exist to serve the industries they're supposed to regulate—and to keep a close watch on consumer-taxpayers who might get uppity ideas about the public interest.

Congressmen serving special interests have been taught the art of slick packaging themselves. Bills have repeatedly been offered to permit price fixing under the name of "fair trade," of "quality stabilization" and other attractively deceptive terms. To the seekers of fixed higher prices, a rise by any other name would be as sweet.

As an example of word juggling, the satellite communications bill (the debate on which was

"WE WANT SOMEBODY TO KEEP AN EYE ON THAT GUY."

5/13/60

"MAN, WE'RE PRESSURE-COOKING ON ALL BURNERS."

6/16/64

"I'M A YOUNG GOIL WHAT WOULD LIKE TO HELP YOUSE WIT' YOUR SHOPPING."

8/18/63

"I'M ALL RIGHT NOW—THIS TIME I'VE CHANGED MY NAME TO BO-PEEP."

9/13/63

"SHH—IF HE SAW ME, IT WOULD ONLY CONFUSE HIM."

4/10/60

"THROW THAT AWAY, GIRL—IT WILL ADDLE YOUR MIND."

7/30/61

never properly reported and publicized) required the satellite corporation to serve the public interest by selling a certain percentage of public stock. Since most stock purchasers have a perfectly natural and proper interest in profits, it hardly follows that the operation of a company which sells stock to the public is necessarily dedicated to the public interest.

A believer in plain, understandable words and figures, Senator Paul Douglas of Illinois has for years urged truth-in-lending regulations which would provide that consumers who make time-payment purchases should, at the very least, know how much they are paying in interest and carrying charges. One opponent of a Douglas bill testified that this would be bad because it would confuse the purchaser. Presumably if a purchaser were to know that he was paying, say, 3 per cent interest a month instead of 3 per cent a year, it would unhinge the poor fellow's reason—and from this kind of dangerous knowledge he must be protected. If there could be such a thing as a pure-motives and truth-in-statements regulation, it would have to exclude as unfit for consumption some arguments which can hardly be swallowed by anyone without gagging.

Advertising and packaging have also been subjects of Congressional inquiries. Some of us have often been a little bewildered to hear about "new, large, giant-size half-quarts" which used to be known simply as pints. But pint-size does not suggest huge quantity. Senator Philip A. Hart's investigation of packaging and labeling of some products disclosed large, giant-size gyps.

Senator Edmund S. Muskie has worked to curb air pollution. So has Senator Maurine Neuberger, who has long fought to require automobile manufacturers to include in their cars modest-priced gadgets which reduce poisonous discharges in the air. Actually such an item, costing only a few dollars, would save the consumer's money as well as his health by providing better consumption of gasoline. But an industry which can provide huge and unnecessary tail-fins, gaudier chrome bumpers and grilles, and everything but silver-plated juke-

"IT TURNS UP IN SOME OF THE JUMBO, GIANT, MORE-COLOSSAL-THAN-EVER CARTONS."

6/29/61

"WHAT! ADD A $10 GADGET LIKE THAT?"

3/4/60

CIGARETTE BOX

1/14/64

"AIN'T IT A BEAUT?"

6/9/63

"I'LL HAVE IT FILLED IN NO TIME."

6/20/62

"YEAH, IT'S ALMOST ENOUGH TO MAKE YOU WANT TO DO SOMETHING."

8/1/62

boxes in its products, screamed with outrage over such proposals.

It was Senator Neuberger also who led the fight to provide health warnings on cigarette packs, a cause which was subsequently taken up by the Federal Trade Commission.

Rachel Carson's *Silent Spring* spurred legislative interest in the control of pesticides whose long-term effects are still under study. But agencies which are more concerned with protecting the public health than protecting industry profits are engaged in a constant battle for support.

One of the most shocking stories in years was the effect of the drug thalidomide, which had been given by some doctors to pregnant mothers, and which resulted in the birth of deformed children. This drug had been kept off the general market in the United States at the insistence of Dr. Frances Kelsey of the Food and Drug Administration, who had been under increasing pressure to remove the restriction—until finally the facts about this drug became public.

The late Senator Kefauver, who had long battled for consumer interests and for greater control of the drug industry, disclosed that quantities of this drug had been distributed by the manufacturer to doctors for promotional purposes, and said that proper tests on animals would have shown the danger of the drug. The thalidomide disclosures were largely responsible for the passage of some of the drug regulation reforms proposed by Senator Kefauver.

But Congress did not adopt his proposals to curb the fantastic profits of some pharmaceutical firms. Many of them have wept about the "costly research" of their work, which sometimes involves the simple duplication and patenting of drug formulas already marketed in other countries. Senator Kefauver also pointed out that no other government grants to individual firms the exclusive manufacturing rights on drugs for the long period of time granted to drug companies in the United States.

Among his many crusades for consumer interests and for honesty in business, Senator Kefauver also brought to light the price-fixing practices among manufacturers of electrical equipment—which eventually resulted in prison sentences for some of the company officials involved.

When some of these men professed complete ignorance of these practices and shock at learning of such goings-on, I thought about the fellow who, according to an old phrase, had played

"MAYBE WE SHOULDN'T HAVE MADE SO MANY SPEECHES ABOUT THE GOVERNMENT SPENDING TOO MUCH MONEY."

3/10/61

"WE ALWAYS INSISTED ON A SALUTE TO THE FLAG."

4/22/61

a piano in a house for many years without knowing what was going on in the upstairs rooms. In the cartoon, I made the character the madam herself; and before running this picture, the editor and I did some wondering about what the reaction from readers would be. There was no criticism, possibly because anyone who might think the setting unsuitable would have had to acknowledge familiarity with it. As a matter of fact, I heard from a few rather distinguished gentlemen who told me they not only recalled the house but thought they recognized a couple of the girls.

The better senators and representatives work constantly to keep each of their respective chambers from being That Kind of House. ■

"GOOD GRACIOUS, YOU MEAN TO SAY SOMETHING'S BEEN GOING ON HERE FOR FIFTY YEARS?"

6/7/61

"SAY, YOU HAVE QUITE A GREEN THUMB."

5/24/59

"WE GENEROUSLY LET YOU PAY FOR THE COW. ALL WE ASK IS THAT YOU LET US TAKE THE CREAM."

9/12/61

"KEEP A CLOSE WATCH ON THOSE MEN OVER THERE–THEY'RE AFTER YOUR MONEY."

9/4/62

"OW! OO! OUCH! HELP! MY TOES!"

2/4/64

"...OUT, OUT, BRIEF CANDLE!
LIFE'S BUT A WALKING SHADOW..."
5/14/63

"SHALL WE RESUME TESTING
HUMAN BEINGS?"
3/22/61

"IT LOOKS LIKE A RAY OF LIGHT
UP THERE."
3/31/60

"SAY, IF WE DON'T GET STARTED
PRETTY SOON–"
6/8/59

10. The Genie and the Bottle

WHITE HOUSE STATEMENT
ON SOVIET RESUMPTION
OF NUCLEAR WEAPONS TESTS
AUGUST 30, 1961

. . . The Soviet government's decision to resume nuclear weapons testing presents a hazard to every human being throughout the world by increasing the dangers of nuclear fallout. . . .

For three years world attention has centered on the negotiations in Geneva for a treaty to secure an end to nuclear testing. Until last March it appeared that slow but encouraging progress had been made. At that time, the Soviet Union reversed its own earlier positions on key issues, refused to discuss seriously the genuine efforts made by the United States and the United Kingdom to meet known Soviet views, and blocked the path toward a nuclear test ban treaty. . . .

STATEMENT BY THE PRESIDENT
ON ORDERING RESUMPTION
OF UNDERGROUND NUCLEAR TESTS
SEPTEMBER 5, 1961

In view of the continued testing by the Soviet Government, I have today ordered the resumption of nuclear tests, in the laboratory and underground, with no fallout. In our efforts to achieve an end to nuclear testing, we have taken every step that reasonable men could justify. . . .

OUT OF THE BOTTLE

9/1/61

THE GOOD EARTH
3/6/59

"THAT'S MY BOY."
6/15/61

"THE QUESTION IS, WOULD IT BE PROPER FOR US TO TAKE SIDES?"
9/24/61

"SLEEP, BABY, SLEEP."
10/25/61

PRESIDENT KENNEDY'S
ADDRESS IN NEW YORK CITY
BEFORE THE GENERAL ASSEMBLY
OF THE UNITED NATIONS
SEPTEMBER 25, 1961

... Unconditional war can no longer lead to unconditional victory. It can no longer serve to settle disputes. It can no longer concern the great powers alone. For a nuclear disaster, spread by wind and water and fear, could well engulf the great and the small, the rich and the poor, the committed and the uncommitted alike. Mankind must put an end to war—or war will put an end to mankind....

* * *

Today, every inhabitant of this planet must contemplate the day when this planet may no longer be habitable. Every man, woman and child lives under a nuclear sword of Damocles, hanging by the slenderest of threads, capable of being cut at any moment by accident or miscalculation or by madness. The weapons of war must be abolished before they abolish us.

Men no longer debate whether armaments are a symptom or a cause of tension. The mere existence of modern weapons—ten million times more powerful than any that the world has ever seen, and only minutes away from any target on earth—is a source of horror, and discord and distrust. Men no longer maintain that disarmament must await the settlement of all disputes—for disarmament must be a part of any permanent settlement. And men may no longer pretend that the quest for disarmament is a sign of weakness—for in a spiraling arms race, a nation's security may well be shrinking even as its arms increase....

The events and decisions of the next ten months may well decide the fate of man for the next ten thousand years. There will be no avoiding those events. There will be no appeal from these decisions. And we in this hall shall be remembered either as part of the generation that turned this planet into a flaming funeral pyre or the generation that met its vow "to save succeeding generations from the scourge of war."

In the endeavor to meet that vow, I pledge you every effort this Nation possesses. I pledge you that we shall neither commit nor provoke

"CAP'N, YOU KEEP CHASING AFTER THAT GREAT WHITE WHALE, WE'RE ALL GONNA END UP IN TROUBLE."

4/29/62

"CLOCK, ANYONE?"

3/15/62

aggression, that we shall neither flee nor invoke the threat of force, that we shall never negotiate out of fear, we shall never fear to negotiate.

* * *

But I come here today to look across this world of threats to a world of peace. In that search we cannot expect any final triumph—for new problems will always arise. We cannot expect that all nations will adopt like systems—for conformity is the jailor of freedom, and the enemy of growth. Nor can we expect to reach our goal by contrivance, by fiat or even by the wishes of all.

But however close we sometimes seem to that dark and final abyss, let no man of peace and freedom despair. For he does not stand alone. If we all can persevere, if we can in every land and office look beyond our own shores and ambitions, then surely the age will dawn in which the strong are just and the weak secure and the peace preserved.

Ladies and gentlemen of this Assembly, the decision is ours. Never have the nations of the world had so much to lose, or so much to gain. Together we shall save our planet, or together we shall perish in its flames. Save it we can—and save it we must—and then shall we earn the eternal thanks of mankind and, as peacemakers, the eternal blessing of God.

CLOUDED CRYSTAL

1/1/62

"YOU MIGHT CALL IT MORE OF AN ABYSS MEETING."

3/11/62

"WHAT WAS ALL THE EXCITEMENT ABOUT ONE MORE NUCLEAR WEAPONS BASE?"

11/4/62

"HOW ABOUT ONE MORE TRY?"

5/29/63

6/14/63

PRESIDENT KENNEDY AT PRESS CONFERENCE,
MAY 8, 1963

Q. Mr. President, would you assume that we will have another round of testing by both the Soviet Union——

THE PRESIDENT. I would think if we don't get an agreement that is what would happen. And I would think that would be... a great disaster for the interests of all concerned. If we don't get an agreement this year... perhaps the genie is out of the bottle and we'll never get him back in again.

RADIO AND TELEVISION ADDRESS
TO THE AMERICAN PEOPLE
ON THE NUCLEAR TEST BAN TREATY
JULY 26, 1963

Good evening, my fellow citizens:

I speak to you tonight in a spirit of hope. Eighteen years ago the advent of nuclear weapons changed the course of the world as well as the war. Since that time, all mankind has been struggling to escape from the darkening prospect of mass destruction on earth. In an age when both sides have come to possess enough nuclear power to destroy the human race several times over, the world of communism and the world of free choice have been caught up in a vicious circle of conflicting ideology and interest. Each increase of tension has produced an increase of arms; each increase of arms has produced an increase of tension.

In these years, the United States and the Soviet Union have frequently communicated suspicion and warnings to each other, but very rarely hope. Our representatives have met at the summit and at the brink; they have met in Washington and in Moscow; in Geneva and at the United Nations. But too often these meetings have produced only darkness, discord, or disillusion.

Yesterday a shaft of light* cut into the dark-

A PLACE IN THE SUN

7/26/63

*The Washington *Post* reprinted this cartoon with the "shaft of light" statement in the text of the President's speech.

ness. Negotiations were concluded in Moscow on a treaty to ban all nuclear tests in the atmosphere, in outer space, and under water. For the first time, an agreement has been reached on bringing the forces of nuclear destruction under international control...

* * *

...this treaty [does not] mean an end to the threat of nuclear war. It will not reduce nuclear stockpiles; it will not halt the production of nuclear weapons; it will not restrict their use in time of war.

Nevertheless, this limited treaty will radically reduce the nuclear testing which would otherwise be conducted on both sides; it will prohibit the United States, the United Kingdom, the Soviet Union, and all others who sign it, from engaging in the atmospheric tests which have so alarmed mankind; and it offers to all the world a welcome sign of hope.

For this is not a unilateral moratorium, but a specific and solemn legal obligation....

...the achievement of this goal is not a victory for one side—it is a victory for mankind. It reflects no concessions to or by the Soviet Union. It reflects simply our common recognition of the dangers in further testing...

* * *

...this treaty can be a step toward freeing the world from the fears and dangers of radioactive fallout...

...The loss of even one human life, or the malformation of even one baby—who may be born long after we are gone—should be of concern to us all. Our children and grandchildren are not merely statistics toward which we can be indifferent.

Nor does this affect the nuclear powers alone. These tests befoul the air of all men and all nations, the committed and the uncommitted alike, without their knowledge and without their consent. That is why the continuation of atmospheric testing causes so many countries to regard all nuclear powers as equally evil; and we can hope that its prevention will enable those countries to see the world more clearly, while enabling all the world to breathe more easily....

...this treaty can be a step toward preventing the spread of nuclear weapons to nations not now possessing them....

In time, it is estimated, many other nations will have either this capacity [to produce and deliver] or other ways of obtaining nuclear warheads, even as missiles can be commercially purchased today.

I ask you to stop and think for a moment what it would mean to have nuclear weapons in so many hands, in the hands of countries large and small, stable and unstable, responsible and irresponsible, scattered throughout the world. There would be no rest for anyone then, no stability, no real security, and no chance of effective disarmament. There would only be the increased chance of accidental war, and an increased necessity for the great powers to involve themselves in what otherwise would be local conflicts.

If only one thermonuclear bomb were to be dropped on any American, Russian, or any other city, whether it was launched by accident or design, by a madman or by an enemy, by a large nation or by a small, from any corner of the world, that one bomb could release more destructive power on the inhabitants of that one helpless city than all the bombs dropped in the Second World War.

Neither the United States nor the Soviet Union nor the United Kingdom nor France can look forward to that day with equanimity. We have a great obligation, all four nuclear powers have a great obligation, to use whatever time remains to prevent the spread of nuclear weapons, to persuade other countries not to test, transfer, acquire, possess, or produce such weapons....

* * *

But now, for the first time in many years, the path of peace may be open. No one can be certain what the future will bring. No one can say whether the time has come for an easing of the struggle. But history and our own conscience will judge us harsher if we do not now make every effort to test our hopes by action, and this is the place to begin. According to the ancient Chinese proverb, "A journey of a thousand miles must begin with a single step."

My fellow Americans, let us take that first step. Let us, if we can, step back from the shadows of war and seek out the way of peace. And if that journey is a thousand miles, or even more, let history record that we, in this land, at this time, took the first step. ■

"COURAGE, MEN, TILL THE CLOUDS COME BACK."

7/28/63

IT'S A WISE FATHER THAT KNOWS HIS OWN BOMB

8/21/63

"WE'VE DECIDED AGAINST THE TEST-BAN TREATY—WE WANT THE RIGHT TO DEVELOP OUR OWN BOMB."

9/15/63

"WE MUST FACE THE UGLY FACT THAT, STEP BY STEP, THIS COUNTRY MAY BE LED DOWN THE ROAD TO PEACE."

9/25/63

"IT'S NOT PRACTICAL—THERE'S NO ASSURANCE THAT IT WOULDN'T ALSO SAVE THE RUSSIANS."

9/12/63

UPI A23N N WA

NIGHT LEAD TREATY

BY WILLIAM THEIS

UNITED PRESS INTERNATIONAL

WASHINGTON, SEPT. 24 (UPI)--THE SENATE TODAY OVERWHELMINGLY RATIFIED THE NUCLEAR TEST BAN TREATY WITH RUSSIA, A HERALDED "FIRST STEP" THAT COULD LEAD TO OTHER TENSION-EASING AGREEMENTS IN THE COLD WAR.

THE HISTORIC ACTION, WITH EVERY SENATOR BUT ONE AILING MEMBER PRESENT, CAME ON A 80-19 ROLL CALL VOTE. THE TREATY BANS NUCLEAR TESTS IN THE ATMOSPHERE, IN SPACE AND UNDERWATER. IT PERMITS UNDERGROUND TESTS.

EVEN AS THE SENATE APPROVED THE PACT, WHICH

CALLED A "SMALL BU

"WITH A GOOD CONSCIENCE OUR ONLY SURE REWARD, WITH HISTORY THE FINAL JUDGE OF OUR DEEDS, LET US GO FORTH TO LEAD THE LAND WE LOVE..."

—John F. Kennedy—Inaugural Address

11/23/63

11. A Time for Living

THE NEWS that came over the air on the afternoon of November 22 was the most shocking that I can remember.

The youngest man to be elected President—he often used the word *hope*, and was himself the symbol of it. He was so able, so keen, with such quick humor and easy gallantry, that the final fact seemed like a denial not alone of life but of the best in living.

I thought back to the freezing January inaugural not even three years before—of the long program, and of the new President's brief speech that was like the flashing of a bright banner; and nothing seemed so fitting as his own brave words.

"I STILL CAN'T BELIEVE IT."

11/24/63

12. Toys in the Attic, the Garage, the Bureau Drawer and Other Easy-to-Reach Places

FOR YEARS the Washington *Post* has been running editorials on the witlessness of permitting the easy, indiscriminate, and unlicensed sale of firearms—particularly pistols, which are designed not for shooting game but for shooting people. And it has also urged sharp restriction of the importation and sale of foreign weapons, such as the one purchased by Lee Harvey Oswald.

Editorials and articles on this subject usually produce reverberations from members of the nearby American Rifle Association, which puts out a publication fully loaded with ads from gun and pistol distributors. These letters of outrage almost always coincide with more news stories of children and adults shooting others dead by accident or in a moment of playfulness or anger. In fact this is almost inevitable, since such killings occur daily. And the range of weapons at hand can be appreciated when we recall an item about some youngsters blowing out the side of a building with a bazooka.

The letters from lobbyists are generally neat, and usually point out that autos also kill people (though autos are not made for this purpose, are not customarily used specifically for killing—and do require a license). These letters nearly always include a stirring reference to the provision in the Bill of Rights that "the right of the people to bear arms shall not be infringed." They do *not* usually include the full brief text of that Second Amendment:

> A well regulated Militia, being necessary to the security of a free State, the right of the people to keep and bear Arms, shall not be infringed.

And never do they mention in what militia all the household pistols and guns we read about are to be employed; in what militia all these children, these impulsive and temporarily crazed adults, are serving or subject to call for duty; against what Indian raids, what buffalo stampedes, what incursions by sailing ships, this militia is to be used. Nor do they explain how, even using the word in its broadest possible definition, such a total-population "militia" could be considered "well regulated" in any sense—except that they may use some TV-advertised laxatives.

The U.S. armed forces, which *are* well regulated, turn down a large percentage of able-bodied men because of illiteracy or low IQ's. But there is no such selectivity for service in the mythical militia of civilian mayhem and murder.

More interesting than the predictable letters from lobbyists and gun-association members are the scribblings that come in from other gun fans and gun fanners, whose childlike printings suggest that they must be slower with the pen or pencil than with the gun. I have often thought that the most effective editorial might be one that consisted solely of a paste-up of such letters. It is enough to give one pause, not to say stop one dead in his tracks, to reflect that the same hand that produces the troubled scrawl about the "rite to shoot a pistel, you Red!" can hold the power to destroy permanently, in a few flashes, friends, strangers, family and neighbors.

The cartoon advertisement—not too different from actual advertisements for such weapons—appeared shortly after the assassination of President Kennedy, and itself became something of

SPORTSMEN!
KIDS! MANIACS!
A whole line of pistols and other weapons, ready to use, including—
this dandy imported rifle, with regular "sharpshooter" telescopic sight
ONLY $12.78
SHIPPED DIRECT TO YOU
ALMOST ANYWHERE IN THE U.S.
Please try not to enclose loose change, to avoid danger of loss.
©1963 HERBLOCK
THE WASHINGTON POST

11/27/63

"HEY, LISTEN—FOR JUST A LITTLE BIT MORE WE CAN GET A REAL ONE."

2/21/64

a target for gun fanciers. Without identifying the gun as the instrument of assassination, I used the gun sight and the price already familiar to newspaper readers because a reporter's research had shown that it was possible to purchase a similar imported gun, with gun sight included, for less than $12.78—the price of the Oswald gun alone.

One newspaper, which seems to be more enthusiastic about guns than about such things as integration or literacy, printed an item pointing out sharply that the gun sight for the Oswald weapon really involved an additional cost!

We often speak contemptuously of countries in which "human life is cheap." Let this not be said about us. Let us by all means have it clear on the record that the cost of the gun that killed the 35th President of the United States was all of $19.95—*with gun sight.*

For those who don't need to be so careful in aim, so selective in target, the friendly shops and mail order businesses offer an even wider variety, with plenty in supply to put guns and lives into the hands of anyone. And the price is right. ■

"HEY, POP,. YOU THINK CIGARETTES ARE REALLY DANGEROUS?"

12/11/63

13. Feature Film...

I DON'T THINK I have a complex about it. I don't feel persecuted or anything. It's just a simple and obvious fact that for many years now the movie exhibitors have been in a conspiracy to keep me from seeing the better films.

They hold back the good ones till I'm up to my ears in work or just about to leave town, and then they let loose a covey of them. Any time I board an outgoing plane and settle back to read the paper, I inevitably see ads for half a dozen great new films and four revivals of classics that I missed the last time around. But you know what happens when I get back to town and have an evening to spend at the movies. Every house in town is showing either *I Was a Teen-Age Monster from Mars* or *Elvis Sideburns Beats the Blues Away*. Or *both together.* With selected short subjects about boy rug-weavers of the Andes, and 30 minutes of "coming attractions."

Those are regular commercial films and theaters I'm talking about. But in 1960 there was produced a Grade Z film that did not appear on the regular movie circuit but was nevertheless one of the most widely seen and talked-about pictures in the country.

The name of this 4-star clinker was *Operation Abolition,* with the catchy subtitle: *The Communist-Led Riots Against the House Committee on Un-American Activities in San Francisco, Calif., May 12–14, 1960.*

Since the bright lights and publicity of show business and movies have always had a particular fascination for this Committee, it was probably inevitable that it should finally become involved with film production itself. This it did with *Operation Abolition*–which must have been almost as low-budget as it was low in other respects, because the Committee subpoenaed the film footage from TV stations, and provided commentary and publicity for it. The Committee then had this unusual film (without any of the usual film credit listings) turned out by a private firm which, within the first few months, sold 700 copies around the country at $100 apiece.

This film was energetically pushed by members of the John Birch Society and Young Americans For Freedom, as well as by veterans' organizations, a number of big industrial corporations, and a variety of civic groups; and pressure from "patriots" resulted in its being palmed off on audiences in schools, PTA's, business groups, clubs, churches, and even departments of the United States Government.

Marquis Childs reported in January 1961:

> In what must surely be one of the most curious transactions ever to have taken place in the huge structure of the Federal bureaucracy, one branch of government is buying a propaganda film from a private firm that obtained the material for the film from another branch of government. The film in question is *Operation Abolition.* . . . This came to light when a Defense Department official sought to interest the Department of State in either borrowing the Defense prints or buying copies of their own. After looking into the circumstances, State Department officials said they were uninterested. A report on the film prepared by the general counsel's office in Defense said that the House Committee seemed to have encouraged the riots with the apparent end of showing how grave the opposition to committee hearings was.

In addition to selected film twists, the movie carried a running commentary by Fulton Lewis III, who was on the Committee's staff at the time, and who described himself as technical director and narrator of the film. This commentary was designed to give the impression (A) that the student demonstrations at the Committee hearings in May 1960 were Communist-inspired, (B) that violence was initiated by students against policemen; and (C) that the policemen were not guilty of brutality.

Of course, the Committee also sought to give the impression that anyone who opposed the Committee must be either a Communist or a Communist dupe. This is standard operating procedure with that group.

The film did indeed show some actual Com-

CUTTING-ROOM FLOOR

11/30/60

munists at the hearings and defying the Committee. They had been subpoenaed to appear before the Committee; and the fact that they were Communists had long been a matter of public knowledge. Some of them mixed with student demonstrators in an effort to achieve publicity and to milk what they could out of the occasion, just as the Committee had scheduled the hearings to get publicity and to milk the occasion for all *it* could.

But no evidence was ever presented that the great body of students were Communists or that their demonstrations were Communist-inspired. Some of the many gimmicks in the film were described by Paul Jacobs in *The Reporter:*

> For example, separate sequences have been run together . . . to give the impression of mob action, and the film shows students displaying defiance after police warnings, although actually the demonstrations occurred at a completely different time. And the police use of fire hoses on the students is justified on the basis of the claim that the students attempted to rush police barricades inside the city hall, where the committee was holding the hearings. But no film accompanies the commentary about the alleged attempt. In fact, photographs taken at the time show the students seated on the floor and in the corridors when the hoses were turned on them.

Among other distortions, the film also gave the impression that Harry Bridges was present before the rioting began, though he did not appear until it was over.

The Chairman of the Committee on Un-American Activities asserted that the film contained absolutely no distortions; but one of the Committee's own investigators had earlier acknowledged on a Los Angeles TV program that the film did contain inaccuracies and distortions. The Committee later conceded that there were some "errors" which it claimed were minor; and a revised version of the film was put out, which contained the same basic distortions as the original.

By the end of February 1961, the National Council of the Churches of Christ issued a statement pointing out that many serious questions were raised by this film, its content and distribution. And the Council advised its constituent communions "not to exhibit the film *Operation Abolition* in churches unless a full and fair presentation of such facts as are available relevant to these questions is provided beforehand and reference made to the National Council's statement." The Council also published an informative booklet on the film, titled *"Operation Abolition: Some Facts and Comments."*

At the same time, such publications as *The Catholic Bulletin* of St. Paul, Minnesota, titled an editorial *"Abolition* Film Dupes Viewers"; and another Catholic publication, the *Oklahoma Courier,* wrote, in an editorial, that

> A movie is being shown locally that was produced with the active help of the House Committee. The name of the movie is Operation Abolition. It contains distortions so blatant and so extreme as to produce the net effect of a lie. The distortions are the result of changing the chronology of the events surrounding committee hearings in San Francisco last May to the extent that the movie fails to be a true account of the actual events.
>
> The Committee's own chief investigator for the West Coast admitted on a television program that the film as edited contains inaccuracies and distortions.

As for the violence on the part of the police, the film sound track said:

> The Communist and pro-Communist press, of course, charge police brutality. Their press accounts of the rioting describe repeated incidents of policemen cruelly beating innocent students. . . .
>
> These films, taken by newsmen on the scene and edited only to the point of removing repetition, show a clear example of the lack of respect for truth, which is common practice within the Communist propaganda press.

But the San Francisco *Chronicle,* which hardly needs to be described as non-Communist, reported in a front-page eyewitness story by George Draper on May 14, 1960:

"THEY'RE *ALL* COMMUNISTS EXCEPT THEE AND ME–"

4/5/61

OPERATION ABOLITION

2/22/61

"YOU TRYING TO UNDERMINE THE AMERICAN WAY OF LIFE?"

6/5/60

"I CAME IN LATE. WHICH WAS IT THAT WAS UN-AMERICAN— WOMEN OR PEACE?"

12/13/62

In December, the Committee on Un-American Activities investigated the organization, Women Strike for Peace.

> They ["about 200 kids"] stood together against the impact of a firehose that splashed against them from above on the landing. There were about 25 blue-uniformed policemen standing like soldiers up there.
>
> The water from the hose cascaded down the stairs, making it as slick as ice. It gushed out into the packed lobby. . . .
>
> I did not see any of the kids actually fighting with police. Their resistance was more passive. They would simply go limp and be manhandled out of the building. At this point it got very tough.
>
> One plump girl was shoved from the top of the stairs and tumbled and slipped down two flights to land like a bundle of clothing at the bottom. The crowd of clerks and civil servants watching broke into a roar of laughter. The girl started to cry.
>
> Another young man, carried bodily by four policemen, kicked out as he went through the big revolving doors at the Polk Street entrance. The glass shattered and tinkled on the marble floor.
>
> "They're using clubs," the crowd screamed. "They're hitting them!"
>
> I saw one slightly built lad being carried by two husky officers. One held the boy's shirt, the other had him by the feet. He was struggling but he was no match for the two bigger men.
>
> Then from nowhere appeared a third officer. He ran up to the slender boy firmly held by the two other officers and clubbed him three times on the head. You could hear the hollow smack of the club striking. The boy went limp and was carried out.
>
> The stairway above me was crawling with people, police and demonstrators in a milling, struggling, screaming, violent mass.
>
> "Don't push me, don't push me!" several girls shouted as they were roughly manhandled by the police.
>
> One pretty coed collapsed at the foot of the stairway. An ambulance steward lifted her eyelids. Her eyes rolled white. "She's alive," he said. He gave her ammonia and then she opened her eyes, frantic with fear, and shrieked.
>
> Police were now clubbing the demonstrators at will.

Another eyewitness, Mel Wax, reported in the New York *Post:*

> Never, in 20 years as a reporter, have I seen such brutality . . . San Francisco police hurled women down the staircase, spines bumping on each marble stair.

Even the film showed the police acting pretty roughly, although it did not show the police clubbing described by eyewitnesses. Nor did it succeed in trying to convey the impression that the students were violent. And it showed nothing at all (much less repetitious) to bear out the statement narrated in this key line:

> One student provides the spark that touches off the violence when he leaps over a barricade, grabs a police officer's nightstick, and begins beating the officer over the head. . . .

It was almost a year after the May 13 uproar in San Francisco that Robert Meisenbach, the student accused of this offense, was tried by a jury and acquitted.

In covering this story, the New York *Post* correspondent reported that police had offered to reduce the charge against the student to a lesser misdemeanor count if the student "would plead guilty and accept a 1-day suspended sentence. He refused." The reporter also noted that "Actually there was no claim made by the police during the trial that Meisenbach was a Communist or a Communist dupe."

The Associated Press story of the same day reported that "Police rebuttal witnesses who assisted in the Meisenbach arrest said they didn't see anybody hit anyone." It also reported of the accusation that a student had leaped a barricade, grabbed an officer's nightstick and started beating him over the head, that "There was no such testimony at the trial."

When I did the Cutting Room Floor cartoon, in November 1960, I received a number of letters from editors as well as readers, demanding to know on what such a cartoon was based; and I replied with excerpts from the film narration and accounts such as that from the San Francisco *Chronicle*. When the movie-award cartoon appeared, following the May 1961 trial (and coincident with the annual Hollywood Oscars) there were no complaints.

There is one more interesting item about the film that cannot be overlooked. In a report by J. Edgar Hoover, titled "Communist Target—Youth" and published by the Committee on

Un-American Activities, in support of its contention that the students were duped, Mr. Hoover had written:

> One of the demonstrators provided the spark that touched off the flame of violence. Leaping a barricade that had been erected, he grabbed an officer's nightstick and began beating the officer over the head....

This was almost word-for-word the same as the line in the film commentary.

And so it turned out that someone had been duped after all—not some young student, but a public official, who, instead of turning up the facts, had parroted a line which was not supported by a single word of testimony under oath.

At last reports the movie was no longer pulling them in, if it was doing any box office at all; and perhaps Mr. Hoover and even the Committee and the distributors would just as soon forget about this once-golden egg.

That's show biz. ■

SPECIAL MOVIE AWARD

5/5/61

14. ...Newsreel...

As a political footnote or down-at-heel-note to the story of the "riot movie" of 1960, the following AP news story of October 1962 is of some interest:

> SAN FRANCISCO, Oct. 4 (AP)—Two Democratic State Assemblymen have denied Richard M. Nixon's charge that they helped lead the riot against the House Un-American Activities Committee in San Francisco in May, 1960.
>
> Assemblymen John O'Connell and Phillip Burton, both of San Francisco, said they were nowhere near the city hall when the riots occurred. Both oppose the committee and had spoken to a students' rally at Union Square the day before.
>
> Mr. Nixon, Republican nominee for Governor, made the charge Monday during a joint appearance with Gov. Edmund G. Brown before an editors' meeting in San Francisco. Departing from the rules, he asked Gov. Brown directly if he were supporting the two...

Mr. Nixon (the old, *old* Nixon and author of a new book about The Six Little Crises and How They Grew) had by 1962 returned to the tactics for which he had become well-known. These were the ones he had employed in the 1954 campaign when he trotted out the old tarbrush and red-paint bucket to ingratiate himself with party hacks by attempting sly smears upon several United States senators. It was at that time that I showed him campaigning cross-country by sewer.

In the 1962 campaign, when he joined once more with his old political campaign partner, Murray Chotiner (whom he had put aside for the Presidential campaign of 1960), and returned to the old tried-and-untrue techniques, I did the together-again cartoon showing him back in his old environment. Later on, in pre-

"YOU FORGOT SOMETHING!"
9/25/62

"OOPS—WRONG BAG OF TRICKS."
3/29/62

convention 1964, he was to speak much of unity—and to achieve unity of a certain kind by creating a sort of national bipartisan consensus on Richard Nixon.

When he was defeated in his 1962 bid for the governorship of California, however, I didn't comment on him at all. But some of his erstwhile friends did.

I said what I had to say about him and them and the responsibilities of the press concerning candidates, in a Columbia University School of Journalism lecture memorializing Elmer Davis, at the beginning of December 1963:

". . . The press often urges voters to take a more active interest in politics and not wait until election day. I would urge the press to do the same thing, not through any means that would diminish its independence, but through its influence *upon* politics.

"Despite the shocking loss of the President, time moves on, an election is coming up next year, primaries are going to be held soon, and already we have seen polls in the papers of the latest comparisons between possible candidates.

"As we enter a new national campaign, I would be interested to know more about what candidates the newspapers themselves prefer. Since the incumbent President is a Democrat and one who seems to have begun very well and would seem to be certain to be nominated by his party, I'm thinking particularly of the Republican press preferences.

"With all the talk about a so-called one-party press, I've never been one who complained about newspapers' expressing honest political preferences, whatever they might be, as long as the publications played fair with the readers. What I *have* objected to is the kind of publication that offers an anonymous mixture of partial news, opinion, propaganda and a few other things.

"I think the press in general might do more than to print and read the polls and take whatever comes up at nominating conventions. And I think they should do some thinking and plain talking about what they want in the way of nominees, and they should do this very soon.

"Roscoe Drummond recently suggested as a Republican Presidential possibility Henry Cabot Lodge—the only new name that's been added recently to the little list of unavowed candidates, in which Richard Nixon's name keeps receiving prominent mention.

"Well, it should not come as a surprise to many of you that I have not been a total admirer of Mr. Nixon, nor an admirer or constant reader of *Time* magazine. *Time* on its part seemed to admire Mr. Nixon greatly—at least up until November 1962, when he lost the governorship race in California.

"In a piece titled 'Career's End,' it said, 'His worst enemies agreed that he was capable, yet they insisted that his character was flawed. As of last week his admirers could only agree.' It ended by saying that his post-press conference remarks left little more to be said about Richard Nixon.

"I couldn't resist peeking into a recent issue of this magazine, to find that more *was* said about Mr. Nixon.

"Accompanying a handsome portrait-type photograph of him, there was an article which did a kind of refurbishing job. And along with this, there was a personal interview in a box. *This* was followed by another piece in the same issue of *Time* which got back on a first-name basis with a reference to 'Dick' Nixon. Whatever the future holds for him, it should always be a comfort to Dick Nixon to know that his old friend 'Hank' Luce never hit him except when he was down.

"You know, old-time newspapermen who wanted us younger fellows to remember the ephemeral nature of our work used to remind us that yesterday's newspaper wraps today's garbage. I think it is Mr. Luce's unique contribution to American journalism that he placed into the hands of the people yesterday's newspaper and today's garbage homogenized into one neat package. . . .

"I've never hoped that either party would nominate some candidate supposedly 'easy to beat,' or would offer as a novel 'choice' the difference, for example, between reason and unreason, or between character and lack of character.

"In the well-remembered TV tour of the White House, Mrs. Kennedy proudly showed the pictures and furnishings and she said that she felt the White House should have the best. I've always felt that both parties should put forward as possible occupants of the White House the *best*. . . .

"I think the newspapers should always make an effort to see that they do, and the press should not be concerned, as politicians often seem to be, with images, with packaging, with political face-lifting. I think newspapers should demand the best in politics, the best of government and of themselves. . . ." ■

15. ...And Selected Short-on-Civil-Liberties Subjects

THESE SHORTS FEATURE SPECIAL SUBJECTS with narrow-screen views.

The Special Effects of blacklisters and censors are darkness and silence. When these cutters of films, books, and careers are tossed out, a couple of loud words are in order: *High time!* When they are nailed, as were the blacklisters of AWARE, Inc., who lost a $3,500,000 libel suit to radio commentator John Henry Faulk, the sound of silence is broken by rousing and fitting cheers.

Save for a few giggles, we can maintain a library quiet as the racists hunt through the shelves, stalking a children's book about a white rabbit who is chummy with a black rabbit. In another library, citizen-censors are agitated about a different relationship—that of Tarzan and his mate.

The practitioners of the Black-Magic loyalty oaths are obviously saying things about the United States Supreme Court which are untranslatable or unprintable. And finally, there is the Wiretapping beast, which is the illegal and unlicensed pet of supposed law enforcement officers. With silent tread, it pads into homes and offices—and keeps trying to creep into law. If this stealthy creature is not curbed, Americans who want to conduct their conversations in privacy may also become more silent. Or they can let out a healthy roar of outrage. ■

"I ENJOYED CENSORING THE MOVIE SO MUCH, ONE OF THESE DAYS I'D LIKE TO CENSOR THE BOOK."
1/26/61

"WHAT ARE YOU DOING? YOU DON'T SEEM TO REALIZE WHO I AM!"

2/12/60

"YOU JANE, ME NEANDERTHAL."

12/31/61

"OH BOY—WAIT TILL THEY DISCOVER 'BLACK BEAUTY.'"

6/3/59

"THIS WILL MAKE HIM A FINE, USEFUL ANIMAL."
7/20/61

OATHS

6/3/64

NAILED

7/1/62

16. Changing World

In my time, I've been married to several barbers. Not with formal ceremonies or anything like that—I just found myself, well, married to them. One at a time, of course.

It's the kind of thing you drift into. You go to a shop in a new neighborhood or dash into one in a downtown hotel, and you take the first barber that's available. I happen to have a soft spot for soft spots, and if the barber lets you settle back and relax in quiet, gives you a good cut, and doesn't wind up covering his mistakes with an application of greasy kid stuff, you figure he's pretty good.

If he's available next time you come to the shop you go to his chair again, even though he may not remember you. But if this keeps on, he *will* remember you. He will even remember when he last cut your hair, and he will look for you.

And then, without knowing how it all came about, you realize that you have become man-and-barber. Gone are the carefree days when you could flit from barbershop to barbershop—or, heaven forbid, from chair to chair. You would no more go to the next barber's chair than you would stroll out of the house after dinner, telling your wife that you were going to spend the night with the divorcee next door.

One time when I had to catch a plane, I sat down in the chair next to the occupied chair of My Barber and smiled as I explained to him that I was in a terrible hurry. He looked at me as if I had stabbed him with his own shears without so much as handing him a styptic pencil.

So you now wait each time for this particular barber—*your* barber—"Fellows, I want you to meet The Little Barber." You make appointments to fit in with his time, and if they interfere with your work schedule, you just rearrange the work, that's all. If he keeps close track, he may even call you and let you know when to come in.

Moreover, the original quiet manner that caused you to return to him in the first place has now been replaced by a garrulous intimacy, which he feels more in keeping with your new relationship. And it would hardly be polite to bury your head in the paper or doze off while he's talking to you. The drowsy hum of the shop's clippers and vibrators is now drowned out by his questions on the most controversial subjects. And he introduces you to his family of other customers, most of whom loathe all your opinions—including the ones he has wrung out of you while you were captive in his chair.

Of course, it's possible to go to another barber—and, in fact, you do when you are on a trip and want a quick trim before appearing at a meeting. But don't think he won't know about it. The next time you see Your Barber, perhaps only in passing on the street, he gives you the Barber's Look. This is a look in the eye—but not quite straight in the eye, because he is also taking in the clipper and scissor work around your ears; and he knows that those ears have been close to scissors and clippers that are not his. At his approach you may have jammed your hat down to eye level. But he *knows*—and he knows just about when it happened. Out-of-town convention—hah! Vacation—ho! He

"TROUBLE GROWING HAIR? YOU CAME TO JUST THE RIGHT PLACE."
8/30/62

9/15/59

7/4/61

9/20/61

"THIS PAIR FEELS PRETTY GOOD."
10/19/62

doesn't say these things, of course; he just gives you the thinnest smile, filled with hurt.

After a meeting like that, there are men who have sheepishly gone back for shearings every four or five days, just to show that everything is as it used to be. But eventually there comes a break. One does not lightly dissolve the bonds that have connected him with one barber chair for years, and barbers long established are not changed for trivial and transient causes; nor does one capriciously put his head into unknown hands that might rub oily gook into it. But somehow the break is made, perhaps while moving to another neighborhood. As a matter of fact, there is no telling how many men have moved to other neighborhoods or skipped town completely just because they found that they had got in too deep with a barber.

It's possible to get in too deep with anything based on habit. And changing habitual views to adjust to new situations can be even harder than changing habits of smoking, drinking, or—or even changing *barbers,* for goodness' sake. But the world changes; and national policies change too.

Through a couple of world wars and postwar periods, we have found ourselves at different times cheering and denouncing the same countries—to name a few: Italy, Turkey, Hungary, Japan, Indonesia, and Russia.

We have also altered our attitudes toward "neutrals"—and the neutrals have often altered *their* attitudes, as well. These changes have not always involved policy flip-flops so much as recognition of changing governments, changing circumstances, or wartime needs.

As people sometimes say, it's a crazy world. But it's not as crazy as it would be if its two greatest powers started lobbing nuclear missiles at each other.

However, there are some who would rather fight than recognize a switch, even though it is a change from the days of nuclear monopoly to a time of possible mutual annihilation.

In the Cuban crisis, when we faced a direct threat that could change the balance of nuclear power, even war was "thinkable." But when Senator J. William Fulbright at a later time suggested that we consider such "unthinkables" as improved relationships with governments that have been at odds with us, some were filled with horror. Many who consider nuclear war "thinkable"—and who even seem to think about it with some relish—find peaceful change too dreadful to think about at all.

If the destruction of the world is thinkable, mutual cooperation is also; and it's something we'd *better* think about. The unhappiest events of the cold war can be remembered without having our minds freeze and our brains congeal into an icy mass incapable of functioning.

I've done a lot of cartoons which were hardly complimentary to Mr. Khrushchev; and many of them appear in this book. The one of Mr. K, Mao, and the UN happened to be printed in the London *Times* while an Anglo-Soviet conference on peaceful coexistence was taking place in London. Robert E. Baker reported in the Washington *Post* that the cartoon brought denunciation from the Soviet delegates in the course of an exchange on free access to foreign publications.

The Soviet delegation insisted that its government had the right to prevent the dissemination of information "not conducive to peace and friendship." And the British pointed out that the Soviets accepted the *Daily Worker* as fitting these standards but that they banned the *Times* and the *Guardian* of Manchester. At this, Georgi Zhukov said "We do not disseminate newspapers which carry such cartoons, for example, as was printed in the *Times* on the opening day of the conference . . ." and, "If such things were turned loose in Russia, we

"LISTEN—WHEN I GET THROUGH WITH IT, IT WON'T BE WORTH BELONGING TO."

2/15/61

"AND STOP PINCHING ME."

5/5/60

would have to strengthen the guard on the British Embassy to protect them against the just wrath of the Soviet public. . . ."

As I recall it, the *Times* the next day gently reminded the Soviets of some of their own cartoons which depicted Uncle Sam and John Bull and American Presidents and British Prime Ministers looking like some less attractive breed of werewolves.

Hungary, the Berlin wall, the resumption of nuclear testing, the slipping of missiles into Cuba while protesting innocence—such things are well remembered by most of us.

But it is not necessary to think of Mr. Khrushchev as an All-American pinup boy to recognize that other and better things have occurred during his regime.

During the Stalin era, it would have been hard to imagine a Communist world in which those who didn't stand shoulder to shoulder were not stood up against a wall.

In the Khrushchev era, when Malenkov, Bulganin and others went out, we waited for the sound of firing squads, but it didn't come. We did, however, hear the shots of sputniks, which demonstrated a high degree of scientific skill. A government in which the loyal or non-loyal opposition was not liquidated was a notable change from the Stalin days.

It would have been hard to imagine, some years ago, a Russian leader denouncing Stalin, citing all his mistakes and cruelties, and having the former idol's body removed from the great tomb in Red Square. It would have been a little difficult also to conceive of Titoism outlasting Stalinism; and of growing independence in some of the satellite countries.

Mr. K has had his troubles with the arts in Russia, and has spoken of modern art as something that looked as if it were daubed with a donkey's tail. He also viewed dimly the political bent of some artists. But similar criticisms of modern artists on both esthetic and political grounds have been made by congressmen in our own country.

Pasternak's famous novel was hardly appreciated. Still, Pasternak was not sent to Siberia; and such writers as the young poet Yevtushenko continued to develop a youthful following, even under Kremlin frowns. The fact is that much of the trouble between Mr. K and the artists and writers has been brought about by the milder policies and the greater freedom of his own regime. As illustrated in one of these cartoons, Pegasus, once allowed to soar, is hard to keep on a short tether.

In recent years there have been more official and unofficial visits between citizens of the U.S. and of Russia. And visitors to the USSR tell me they now have greater freedom of movement, more opportunities to get about without

"AH, YES—WE HAVE MANY THINGS IN COMMON."

7/2/59

ONE-MAN SHOW

3/13/63

"ONWARD AND UPWARD, BUT NOT TOO FAR."
5/9/63

"WE ARE NOT A MUSE."
4/12/63

guides and to visit the homes of Russian people than they had several years ago. There has also been more trade with Russia, and the beginnings of independent agreements with non-Russian members of the Communist bloc.

The wheat deal with Russia induced in some people here a kind of Pavlov reaction which involved not so much salivation as frothing at the mouth. It certainly did not alarm me. Peace, as well as an army, moves on its stomach; and when the stomach is full of food, there is less stomach for war.

The Russian increase in consumer goods is also dandy with me. In the early thirties it was said that the most devastating thing we could do to the Soviet government would be to drop Sears-Roebuck catalogues all over Russia. I think that even better than that would be to have all the products in those catalogues available to the Russian people—and produced in factories devoting their full efforts to peaceful goods.

It was this very turn toward consumer welfare in the USSR that produced some of the most biting blasts from China, where Mr. K is regarded as being soft-on-capitalism—or if I

"PSST—WANT TO SEE SOME POEMS?"
10/17/61

remember the news story translation from the Chinese correctly: a psalm-singing Bible-reading capitalist capitulationist.

Who would have thought a few years back that there would not only be more freedom of operation for some of the Russian satellite countries, but also the most bitter exchanges with Communist China? But such significant and perhaps world-shaking changes seem to have little meaning for the Neanderthals who recognize no changes anywhere. To them communism is communism and capitalism is capitalism—and never the twain shall meet, except in war.

It's probably significant that many of those who are least willing to recognize change in the world are also least willing to recognize it in our own country—and least want it. Inflexible opposition to civil rights legislation, to the Supreme Court, to the Federal government, are not entirely unrelated to an inflexible stance in the world. Some of the same people who regard it as unthinkable that the cold war can in time be terminated, seem also most determined to keep alive the Civil War.

There are, of course, irreconcilables and war whoopers in the Communist world also; and Mr. Khrushchev has stood up to them. On one occasion, when he was touring Hungary in the spring of 1964, the Soviet Premier served up a statement about goulash, which contained some hot pepper for his Chinese critics.

"There are some people in the world calling themselves Communists," he said, "...who do not consider it important to strive for a better life, but call only for the making of revolution." He went on to assert that the aim of revolution was higher living standards, including "good goulash," along with such things as better clothing, housing, education and culture.

"Good goulash," or "goulash and ballet," may not seem to have the ring of "Life, Liberty and the Pursuit of Happiness," but it can well be as revolutionary in its way—and for a large part of the world a declaration of independence from the bonds of dialectic dogma.

I don't suggest that we should toss away our arms, accept at face value everything put out by the Soviet government, or assume that there will be no more difficulties, threats, dangers or even deceptions. I *do* suggest that there have been changes in the world—particularly in the Communist world and in Russia itself. I suggest that it is possible to live in peace and to continue to reach better understanding; that in the face of Chinese threats, we and the Russians may be drawn still closer together; and that the Communist countries may move closer to our way of life.

This, however, will not happen if the why-not-victory and no-negotiation-till-they-surrender boys in our country and in China can help it.

I can see the brows of our hardheads darkening at the very mention of coexistence. They regard such talk as a barber regards an old customer who has defected to another chair. Improvement in Communist Russia? Anything in the world worse than Communist Russia? What outrageous thoughts!

But wait—there are words and precedents that even these men might recognize. It was pointed out in a Washington *Evening Star* editorial of June 26, 1962, that

> ...what ought to be remembered by the Republicans is that the late Secretary of State Dulles, as far back as 1956, spoke of the "yeast of freedom" at work in the USSR, and predicted a great and beneficent international transformation by 1965...

This, incidentally, was cited by the *Star* in chastising "men like Senator Goldwater" who "seize upon undocumented news stories to accuse the Democrats of appeasing the Reds."

What a coincidence that less than five months before 1965, this same Senator Goldwater, proclaimer of a total-victory, total-Communist-surrender policy, was saying that he followed the policy of the late Secretary Dulles. It is too bad that this candidate, in speaking of Dulles' policy, did not consider (to coin a phrase) "the whole man"—the prophetic "yeast of freedom" Dulles, as well as the "brinkmanship" and "massive retaliation" Dulles.

But perhaps even more impressive are the statements of the Senator himself, who cited such organizations as the American Civil Liberties Union as being among the greatest threats to the nation; who expressed more fear of "Washington and centralized government" than of Moscow; and who said that "Walter Reuther is more dangerous than the sputniks or anything Russia might do."

So it is possible for something or somebody, right here in our own country, to be more dangerous than Russia. The disagreement then is only on *what* or *who.*

My opinion is that the greater menace is the kind of trigger-happy politician who lacks the responsibility or the brains to recognize what both the President of the United States and the Premier of Soviet Russia have had the sense and the courage to tell their people—that in nuclear war there can be no winner, and that the danger of such a war is one we must both avoid by every means possible.

One close shave is enough. ■

"COME ON, COME ON—DON'T BE A COWARD."

1/3/63

ROOF OF THE WORLD
11/30/62

"SMALL WORLD, ISN'T IT?"
10/9/63

"OH DEAR–SOMETIMES I THINK THEY'RE NOT EVEN LISTENING."
4/23/60

"THIS CONCLUDES ANOTHER LESSON IN COMMUNIST COOKING."
7/12/61

3/20/62

"SINCE YOU'VE BEEN GOING WITH THAT DOLL, YOU'RE GETTING CHICKEN."
12/16/62

"DEAR FRIEND AND COMRADE: WE LONG TO WELCOME YOU AGAIN. LET US HEAR FROM YOU SOON, ADMITTING THAT YOU ARE A NO-GOOD, TWO-FACED, LOUSY BUM.
P.S. YOU RAT!"
2/28/63

"NO, *YOU* BE *OUR* GUEST."
4/3/63

COLD LINE
5/11/63

"IT'S PEACEMONGERING AND CREEPING PRIVATE ENTERPRISE, THAT'S WHAT IT IS!"
10/11/63

"PSST! WANT TO SEE SOME HOT STATISTICS?"
1/17/64

"MAN, THAT GUY IS WEIRD."

3/29/64

"IT'S A RELIEF TO GET RID OF THE OVERCOAT."

4/22/64

"VERY CLEVER. THAT SHOULD GIVE BOTH OF THEM TROUBLE AT HOME."
2/7/64

DARKNESS AT HIGH NOON
4/7/64

"THAT'S HOW DECADENCE SETS IN—FIRST HE'S IN FAVOR OF LIVING, AND NOW *BETTER* LIVING."
4/12/64

"HELL, I THOUGHT HE SAID DES*TALIN*IZATION."
6/24/64

17. Readin' and Riotin'...

WHEN I read today about the problems of school financing, school enrollments, school and teacher shortages, schools and poverty, sex, violence and whatnot, I drift back occasionally to a time when school problems were personal ones; when school and home comprised a small world. Actually, they comprised two small worlds, bridged by playmates, homework, report cards, and an occasional note from home explaining that Herbert was absent yesterday because he had to go to the dentist.

This seemed to me to be all the communication between those worlds that was necessary or desirable, and I directed some effort to maintaining the status quo.

At that time the PTA had not reached full flower, but there were the beginnings of it in what were called "Parents' nights," kind of open-house evenings at school. These occasions I usually neglected to mention at home; and on those evenings I generally found some dandy movie that I thought my parents might like to see.

Without having learned much of government or diplomacy, I had a certain basic idea: that parents, fine as they were, represented Authority; that teachers, however good, also represented Authority; and that a coalescing of these forces might result in a combination of power too great for the general welfare of one little kid.

Undoubtedly, one reason I discouraged my parents from visiting school was because of the practice, perhaps still prevalent, of emblazoning on the blackboard of each room a large "Honor Roll" of students who were Very Good to Excellent in every subject. These Honor Rolls were usually done with drawings of scrolls, sunbursts, eagles, and stars in six colors of chalk; and if neon tubing had been available, that would have been used too. So if my parents had entered that room it would have been impossible for them to miss this blackboard technicolor "spectacular," or to have avoided noticing that their boy's name not only did not lead all the rest but was rarely on that list at all.

Most of us who devoted our modest drawing abilities to cartoons and posters regarded the students who contributed their artistic talents to illuminating these Honor Rolls as a bunch of finks, betraying their schoolmates and prostituting their art.

There have been many changes since then, and today meetings between parents and teachers are more frequent, more helpful, and less fearsome to all concerned. As for report cards, if a term like "group adjustment" is something of a euphemism, it is probably, for the student, an improvement over the word "deportment"—which was so easy to understand and in which the grades were sometimes so difficult to explain.

Having noted the customary concerns of schoolchildren, or at least many of them of my generation, I ought to add that I really found a great deal of pleasure in the public schools. The fact is that in a day when cartoons and writings generally depicted red-blooded American boys as hating school and loathing teachers—a holdover, probably, from the days of hickory-stick teaching and nearby swimming holes—I felt a little secret guilt about *liking* school.

By now those old clichés should be pretty dead; and even in popular mythology schools can no longer be regarded as dread places. As a number of education and welfare experts have noted, in many areas today the school is the only hopeful spot, the only bright center of activity, the only chance to find a way out of areas of complete blight and lives of utter squalor—and it is in those areas that we need the best schools and the best teachers.

During the past several years, anyone who has read news stories from Alabama, Mississippi, and many places farther north, must be aware of the fact that for millions of Americans the chance for an adequate education has been a bright but unrealized dream.

The National Committee for the Support of Public Schools, founded by Agnes E. Meyer, has done a great deal of public educating *about* education. It has tried to light fires of interest in communities across the country, and on occasion some of its members have applied the warm lamp of learning to a few seats of power.

"WE CAN'T BURDEN OUR CHILDREN WITH DEFICIT SPENDING."

1/31/63

OLD MAN AND THE SEA
8/24/61

Many affluent adults, however, are still below passing grade in the mathematics and economics of education. Some still think that schools can be supported, as of old, by real estate taxes alone. They have failed to note the multiplication of people and the fact that the tax-dollar pie is no longer divided as it used to be. Otherwise bright and influential citizens have yet to establish the connection between ignorance and poverty, education and employment, purchasing power and prosperity. And a special class, who might be called the retarded rich, has never learned about such simple fractions as "the other half."

A report by Mrs. Meyer's committee titled "The Businessman Looks at Education" showed that among influential laymen there has been a great and growing awareness of the importance of education. However, the excerpts from comments by some of these men (with names deleted) showed that there are, as in every group, always a few who don't get the word.

Among the many interesting statements by businessmen, one could not help doing a double-take at the comment of *Aircraft Company Executive,* who is probably working constantly for faster jet planes, but who says of school

"WHEN DO YOU THINK THERE'LL BE SOME EXCITEMENT ABOUT SCHOOL *DIS*INTEGRATION?"
8/31/58

"IT'S NOT THE PRINCIPLE – IT'S THE MONEY."
2/11/59

progress, "Granted progress is slow, but I feel this is proper."

And then there is a response from *President, Power Company,* who fears that schools are "moving too far from basics and fundamentals, resulting in too heavy a financial burden" and that we should eliminate the "frills" and save money by getting back to the "little red schoolhouse."

This fellow is right out of an executive coloring book. We could add a few billions to the green money we would save by getting back to the little red schoolhouses, and could build bigger and grayer jails, reformatories and workhouses—and color the future dark.

The future is brighter for the work that conscientious citizens have been doing for education.

It is brighter by far for the beacon-light decisions of the United States Supreme Court. It is brighter for the lamps lit by Presidents Kennedy and Johnson to provide educational opportunities for children twice deprived: first,

"WANT TO TRANSFER TO MY SCHOOL, KID?"

8/4/63

"THE DELINQUENCY PROBLEM MUST BE FACED—WE'VE GOT TO BUILD MORE JAILS."

1/27/63

because of their color; second, because of the burden of ignorance and poverty so long laid upon their families.

For seven years after the Supreme Court decision of 1954, groups opposed to equal education grew like tumors while a Chief Executive lamented that you can't change the hearts of men by laws—and showed the heart for neither the legal nor the moral challenge of the times.

Desegregation progress has been deliberately, drearily slow. But if ten years have been a long time, the era before the Court decision seems like a remote age.

One of the most interesting features of this time has been the influence of state and local leadership on desegregation—including the role of the press, which has shown that it is still a great force for good when it engages in great causes.

In most cities the progress of desegregation has seemed to be more closely related to the conscience and courage of newspapers and local officials than to geography or population percentages by races. In Atlanta and Louisville, for example, great papers under great editors informed the people and prepared them for change. This compares sharply with the violence in Birmingham and the massive ignorance and prejudice fostered in Richmond, Virginia—a little bit north of North Carolina, which has a better and more responsible press that has made its contributions to the welfare of a more enlightened state.

Dante said that the hottest places in Hell are reserved for those who, in a time of great moral crisis, maintain their neutrality.

In my own little Inferno there are public accommodations for those who would deny accommodations to others, plenty of room for mobs to mill around, and certainly special circles for those who live in the best circles but can never raise their voices against outrages. But editorially, the lowest level and the warmest flames must be reserved for those who work at the basest level and who themselves fan the flames of prejudice and fear to serve their own ends.

In Little Rock, Arkansas, in 1957, the schools could well have been integrated without incident. But even a fine newspaper under a courageous editor could not stop a Governor,

"I THINK THIS IS RATHER A SAD SORT OF THING . . ."

12/11/58

"A FUNNY THING HAPPENED ON THE WAY TO KICKING OUT 1000 SCHOOL KIDS—"

5/24/63

"...HE TOOK WATER AND WASHED HIS HANDS BEFORE THE MULTITUDE..."
10/3/62

"FELLOW IN MISSISSIPPI IS DETERMINED TO ENROLL HERE. SHALL WE LET HIM IN?"
9/28/62

determined to advance his own political interests, from calling out troops to prevent orderly desegregation.

Mississippi's former Governor Ross Barnett will never quite get his hands clean from the night's work he helped inspire at the University of Mississippi, when a mob attacked U.S. Marshals, and when two nonparticipants, one a foreign newspaper correspondent, were killed. Barnett has a special place in my little Inferno—and he put himself in a good position for a place in a Federal penitentiary.

Governor Wallace of Alabama, a politician who had calculated that the easiest road to success for him was to "out-seg" the other segregationists in his state, went through his little charade of standing at the University door and then posting troopers at schoolhouse doors. If those Alabama voters who gave this political delinquent his small election majority did not feel that their intelligence was insulted by this kind of hamming, then additional schools in Alabama are even more badly needed than most of us had supposed.

It has been at the lower grade school levels that the white supremacists have been at their own abysmally lowest grade. The banshee cries

"HELP!"
11/16/60

"BAD NEWS, CHIEF–EDUCATION IS BREAKING OUT IN ANOTHER AREA."
9/4/63

"WELL, I TRIED TO BLOCK THE DOORWAY."
6/12/63

"I DON'T WANT ANY INSIDE INTERFERENCE!"
9/8/63

"THIS IS THE END OF ANTI-CIVILIZATION AS WE'VE KNOWN IT."

5/26/64

of New Orleans women who shrieked at Negro children on their way to school died down after a term. But in a special class, because for four years it had no public school classes at all, was the case of Prince Edward County, Virginia. The Byrd machine and its journalistic camp followers in Richmond had been forced to abandon the much-heralded policy of "massive resistance" to the original Court school decision. But as a final defiant gesture, the public schools of Prince Edward County were kept closed—on a "local option" basis, of course—while the state and county aided "private schools" for white children.

In 1963, Attorney General Kennedy pointed out that there were, outside of Africa below the Sahara, only five places in the world where free basic education was not offered to the children of a country: Communist China, North Viet-Nam, Sarawak, North Borneo, and Prince Edward County, Virginia.

Later that year, free schools were established in Prince Edward, largely through the work of William vanden Heuvel, Special Assistant to the Attorney General, who enlisted the aid of private foundations and public leaders.

When schools were set up in that area to accommodate the children cheated of four years of education, some of these youngsters had to be taught even how to hold a pencil.

Newspaper reporters who went there when the free schools began found families where the children were so excited they hadn't been able to sleep. The reporters saw children up to nine, ten and eleven years of age, who had risen at dawn and dressed in their meager best, awaiting the supreme moment of their lives—the chance to enter a schoolroom!

The action of the Byrd politicians in Virginia in giving vent to their hatred of the Supreme Court and of the United States government by taking it out on the children—on the humblest and poorest and most helpless and neediest of the children—surely stands as one of the most wanton and cruel acts ever performed by any political machine in the entire history of our nation.

When the Supreme Court, in June 1964, brought an end to this oldest desegregation case and ruled that the schools must be open to all, Senator Byrd dropped the velvet glove and showed his own heavy hand by personally attacking what he kept referring to as "the Warren court" for "this latest dictatorial act."

TEN
"I'M ~~EIGHT~~. I WAS BORN ON THE DAY OF THE SUPREME COURT DECISION."

5/17/64

Thus spoke Boss Byrd whose political machine reduced the once proud state of Virginia to one of the most backward states of the Union, and operated it as a feudal serfdom.

Slowly, the bastions of ignorance have been crumbling. And in all their bitter denunciations of the Supreme Court it is possible that the Byrds, the Barnetts, the Eastlands and Wallaces, are really less fearful of the Supreme Court than of another institution—the school itself, the free, open-to-all school. The racist demagogues and rulers of state fiefdoms need not send to know for whom the school bell tolls. It tolls for them. ■

"I CAN'T COME OUT AND RIOT
TONIGHT–I GOT TO STUDY CIVICS."

11/29/62

"GEE, IF ONLY WE COULD HAVE CLOSED THE COURTS."

9/18/58

HIGHER EDUCATION IN MISSISSIPPI

10/2/62

OTHER FOREIGN NEWS

10/26/62

"IF PEOPLE GET EDUCATED, AND IF THEY CAN VOTE, WHAT'S TO BECOME OF US?"

4/4/63

18. ...And Religion

For anything so closely associated with tranquillity of spirit and peace of mind, religion certainly has a remarkable capacity for raising the blood pressure of the body politic. Within a period of two or three years beginning in 1960, tempers rose over *(1)* a Presidential candidate's religion, *(2)* Federal aid to religious schools, and *(3)* religious recitations in public schools.

In each of these situations there were paradoxes to make W. S. Gilbert giddy. Few people are more determined to inflict their will on others than those who most zealously proclaim that all matters rest in the hands of a Supreme Being; and many a holy crusader marches forth clad in the heaviest irony.

In 1960, Presidential candidate John F. Kennedy found himself opposed by some of the most influential American figures of his own church—as did another political candidate, Governor Luis Muñoz-Marin of Puerto Rico, who was the target of a pastoral letter issued by three Puerto Rican bishops.

With the election of President Kennedy, who stood for increased Federal aid to education, hopes for a comprehensive public school aid bill blossomed—until they were chilled by a drive for Federal aid to religious schools. On this point Mr. Kennedy faced from many members of his own faith pressure greater than they had tried to exert on his Protestant predecessors. A firm believer in separation of church and state, President Kennedy resisted the pressure; but in Congress, Federal aid to elementary and secondary schools was once more stymied.

My own feeling about religion and government is that the combination is one that calls for the same admonitions we receive about driving and drinking or Smokey Bear's forests and lighted matches.

To those who argue, on behalf of government funds for parochial schools, that "*Our*

"WE DIDN'T DO SO WELL EITHER."

11/11/60

"THIS LITTLE KID'S GOT A BIG GUY WITH HIM."

2/21/61

"LONG TIME NO SEE."
9/6/60

children are entitled to an education too," I say —if the expression is not inappropriate—Amen. I'll get in there and pitch for any child who is being denied schooling, whatever his race, color or religion. But when a public school is open and parents choose to send their children to a private school instead, I don't see how those children are being denied an education or denied any rights. And it seems ironic indeed that some people in effect feel discriminated against for lack of government-supported separate-but-equal religious schools, when real victims of discrimination have finally won recognition of the fact that schools which are separate are not equal.

If the public and parochial schools were equal except for some additional religious training, the solution would seem to be quite simple and a great saving of expense to religious schools: Those who wanted the extra religious training could get it through a little after-public-school time at church schools that devoted themselves exclusively to such training.

As for the argument that religious schools save the government money on public schools, this "saving" is one which the aid-to-religious-school advocates would curtail. But more importantly, the same argument could be advanced on behalf of any other type of private school, as well as many private libraries, private

"HERE, LITTLE BOY, PULL THE NICE HORSIE IN WITH YOU."
3/8/61

2/12/63

"NICE KITTY CAN'T COME IN?"
6/27/62

"HANG ON A WHILE LONGER—
I'LL SAVE YOU."
5/5/64

"I'LL GET YOU IN THERE IF
IT KILLS YOU."
5/10/64

"EVERY SCHOOLCHILD SHOULD BE
MADE TO PRAY AGAINST
GOVERNMENT INTERFERENCE
WITH PRIVATE LIVES."
6/2/64

art collections—or, for that matter, on behalf of private fire protection, private police guards and similar special services.

But it is not argued that government should contribute to the pay of private detectives, for example—however useful some of their work may be—as long as there is a public police force with its own detective bureau. Special private services beyond those provided in public facilities are paid for privately and separately. And of all things private and personal, religious education would seem to be the one thing that no one should want to see dependent on the giving or withholding of government funds.

The loudest boom for the combustible mixture of religion and government has come from politicians who have railed against the Supreme Court's school prayer decision, and have made the wall of separation between church and state their personal wailing wall. And curiously enough, these include a lot of the same politicians who deplore all public welfare measures and see in each a plot by an octopus-like government to reach into private affairs.

Impoverished children in the districts of some of these anti-welfare politicians might feel a kinship with the homeless boy, Jo, in Dickens' *Bleak House*. When asked, as he lay dying, "Jo, did you ever know a prayer?" he answered:

> No, sir. Nothink at all. Mr. Chadbands he wos a-prayin wunst at Mr. Sangsby's and I heerd him, but he sounded as if he wos a-speakin' to hisself, and not to me. He prayed a lot, but *I* couldn't make out nothink on it. Different times, there was other genlmen come down Tom-all-Alone's a-prayin, but they all mostly sed as the t'other wuns prayed wrong, and all mostly sounded to be a-talking to theirselves, or a-passing blame on the t'others, and not a-talkin to us. *We* never knowd nothink. *I* never knowd what it wos all about.

In the long-ago days when I attended public schools, there were two things we knew by heart and used to recite regularly. One was the Preamble to the Constitution, in which we raised our small voices to "insure domestic Tranquility, provide for the common defence, promote the general Welfare . . ." Of course, we were just kids, and we didn't know, any more than the founders of the Republic knew, that *Welfare* would come to be regarded by some Americans as a dirty word.

The other thing we recited was the pledge of allegiance to the American flag, "and to the Republic for which it stands, one Nation, indivisible, with liberty and justice for all."

Since then this pledge has been amended, somewhat awkwardly, to say "one Nation, under God, indivisible . . ."

In our earlier day we thought the original form was all right. We didn't mean any harm. We didn't know that God might get sore and strike us all dead for failing to give Him a plug in that pledge. We didn't even know that He needed the publicity—or that He needed to be reminded daily that our territory came under His jurisdiction.

Those who keep a sharp eye on the children to see that they don't get by just with being good students needn't stop with the change already made in the pledge.

There is no reason to let the kids get away with the simple declaration "I pledge allegiance . . ." This could be changed to "I, Johnny Jones, who am not now and never have been a member of any subversive organization, pledge allegiance . . . "

The word *republic* is okay with the Birchers, who don't like the word *democracy*. But with some States' Righters, *indivisible* will have to go.

And at the conclusion, the words "with liberty and justice for all" might be followed by reservations to explain that this does not necessarily include those too poor to afford education, bail or legal fees—and certainly not all those of any old race or color.

In time sufficient amendments might be added to this pledge to close any possible loopholes—and to close some young minds as well.

However, the big effort recently has not been for change in minor things like the pledge, but for amending the Constitution itself to provide for religious observance in schools—even though it would nullify the first Article in the Bill of Rights.

If you can believe it, the argument has been advanced with a straight face that freedom of religion does not mean freedom *from* religion. Since the First Amendment also guarantees freedom of the press, it might as logically be argued that *this* provision does not mean freedom *from* the press, and that therefore everyone should be required to be a writer or publisher—or at least a subscriber. Everyone could then be obliged to subscribe to a publication *and* a religious belief.

One congressman has spoken of the need to make sure that every child knows there is a God. In the early days of my life, such Americans as Mark Twain and Thomas A. Edison did not profess to know about that. And the most devout religious leaders have spoken in terms of faith. But some of the politicians *know*.

I envy these congressmen their intimacy with God. They know all about Him, and what denomination He belongs to, and what He wants done, and how He wants to be addressed. And they are going to save Him by putting Him in the public schools. This is very generous of them. They are busy and important men.

I can't help noting, however, that many of the congressmen who are hellbent for religion in the public schools have never been much for *education* in the schools.

Many of these pious politicians have never been much concerned about children getting part-time education, or about children being denied educational opportunities altogether. But to hear these men weep and carry on about how the children are being, as they put it, "denied the right to pray," you'd think all the homes and churches and Sunday schools had been closed, and the kids were in school under lock and key 24 hours a day.

At the time of the Supreme Court's prayer decision, President Kennedy suggested, in answer to a question, that those who were dissatisfied with the Court's ruling on prayers in school might do more praying at home and in churches. One Washington reporter, upon making a few inquiries in the days following President Kennedy's observation, found nothing to indicate that there had been any increase in such out-of-school praying.

The attitude of some school-religion advocates seems to be that the schools provide a convenient dumping ground for everything. Prayer in school or on "released time" from school is all right. But provide religious training in "re-

**"WHAT DO THEY EXPECT US TO DO—
LISTEN TO THE KIDS PRAY AT *HOME?*"**
6/18/63

leased time" from home TV-watching or record-playing? What are you, a religious *fanatic?*

Of course, what many politicians and other people are talking about is not their own children but *other* people's children. They want to make sure that everybody believes—no, that everybody *knows*—as they know, even though they may not be able to agree on a common prayer or reading or recitation to express precisely what it is that all of them believe—that is, *know*.

While these people are considering appropriate readings on religion, let me suggest a couple for them. The first is from Thomas Jefferson:

> I have considered religion as a matter between every man and his Maker, in which no other, and far less the public, has a right to intermeddle.

But if they don't care for Jefferson as an authority, they can go directly to the New Testament and one of the greatest of all religious passages, in which the multitude is told:

> . . . when thou prayest, thou shalt not be as the hypocrites are: for they love to pray standing in the synagogues and in the corners of the streets, that they may be seen of men. . . .
>
> But thou, when thou prayest, enter into thy closet, and when thou hast shut thy door, pray to thy Father which is in secret. . . .

And:

> . . . when ye pray, use not vain repetitions, as the heathen do: for they think they shall be heard for their much speaking.

I commend to the chaplains on both sides of the Capitol these passages from the Sermon on the Mount for reading aloud to their little multitudes on the "Hill."

There are those who would convert a world struggle for individual freedom into a kind of "holy war" in which the difference between us and the totalitarians would be not that we were free but that we were religious—forgetting that while free governments have protected religion,

"LEAVING RELIGION TO PRIVATE INITIATIVE IS UN-AMERICAN."

6/28/62

religious governments have seldom protected freedom—or freedom of religion.

Many "honest, Godfearing" people have been caught up in this religious-crusade idea much as they were caught up in McCarthyism, and for much the same reason—the hope that we can defeat communism through some exorcism of devils at home, or through magic incantations. I use the word "incantations" without irreverence, because the religion-in-school advocates seem less interested in prayer from within than in the mechanical recitation of prayer, like the spinning of Tibetan prayer wheels.

As the 1964 hearings on the school-prayer amendment went on, more and more religious leaders of all faiths spoke up against it, as contrasted to some of the political religionists and religionist politicians who had been heard from earlier. In a survey in the spring of '64 conducted by the national magazine of the Holy Cross Fathers, 35 of 48 editors of Catholic publications said they were against the proposed school-prayer amendment. And in June, the Associated Press reported that the National

"WHAT ARE YOU GUYS—A BUNCH OF ATHEISTIC COMMUNISTS OR SOMETHING?"

6/28/64

Catholic Welfare Conference, whose position it described as coming "close to being an official statement by the U.S. Roman Catholic Hierarchy," advised extreme caution toward the proposed amendment and called the existing clauses of the First Amendment "of incalculable benefit."

Along with the sincere expressions of opinion on both sides of the school-prayer issue, and the opportunism of some politicians who wanted to climb aboard a proposal that was bringing in mail from home, there has been an uglier aspect to this controversy—the attempt of segregationists to whip up fervor for the prayer amendment as a way of lashing the Supreme Court for its earlier rulings on equal rights.

Such men would press God into political service to spearhead their shabby crusade against the Supreme Court of the United States. Actually, they would reverse Biblical procedure and create God in their own image—a white and hate-filled God.

One Southern congressman cracked that "The Supreme Court put Negroes into the schools, and now it has taken God out." It can be said of many of the white supremacists who gleefully repeated this phrase that they never wanted Negroes or Christian spirit in their schools *or* their churches. And during the same hot summer that the school-prayer amendment was in the news, it was even bigger news when the UPI reported from racist-ridden St. Augustine, Florida, that "An Episcopal rector today personally escorted five Negroes into his church for the first time."

So the motives of some of the pious politicians have been as plain as black and white.

And what about those sincere, devout people who honestly believe that the government should finance or sponsor religion or put it into the public schools? To convert these people and satisfy everyone, I have a simple if somewhat unusual plan. It requires only some high U.S. official—perhaps one who is ready to retire anyhow—willing to sacrifice himself on behalf of public understanding.

The high official would proclaim that not only was it important for the government to foster religion but that religious training was of such *transcendent* importance that it could no longer be left to private hands, to hit-or-miss religious efforts, or to the risk of the wrong kind of indoctrination. He might even spell it out

"PRAY KEEP MOVING, BROTHER."
8/14/60

"MAYBE WE OUGHTA CLOSE THEM TOO."
11/23/58

"YOU KNOW WHAT I'D LIKE TO DO? I'D LIKE TO PUSH THIS RIGHT DOWN OVER THAT GUY'S EARS."
12/15/60

further by saying that the churches had better keep in line with the government effort or close up; and he could suggest that kids snitch to the government on parents who tried to take religion into their own hands at home.

The whole thing, he would point out, would need to be coordinated from Washington.

That would do it. The results would be instantaneous. From one end of the land to the other, Americans would rise up to denounce the official and to cry out against the government. Prayer meetings would be held continuously, and the churches would be packed to the lofts with defiant, freedom-loving Americans, while overflow crowds trampled the grass, the flowers and the grapes of wrath. Others would gather in public squares to proclaim themselves agnostics or atheists, defy the government to do its worst, and call for "liberty or death." Parents who had never before bothered about such matters would bravely hold Bible readings in their homes; they would have the children join them in prayer morning and night and at every meal, with special religious observances on weekends and holidays.

The entire nation, members of all faiths and those of no faith, would be united in one common goal—the preservation of religious freedom. And no one would rest until the Monstrous Threat from Washington had been hurled back, and the high public official driven from the capital.

Public demand would force withdrawal of all religious observance in the public schools. And once in motion, there's no telling how far such a reaction would carry. There might be a general demand that "In God We Trust" be removed from our coins as representing a profane kind of sloganeering. There might even be harsh comments about politicians who drag in God to wind up all their speeches.

We would then be back to the old days—back about where the Founding Fathers came in, when memories of religious conflicts were fresher—all of us feeling more as the Founders did then, when they "left God out" of the Constitution and established a government that forbade establishment of religion. For, as wise clergymen and judges have pointed out over a long number of years, when a free government mixes in religion, it's a bad day for freedom—and for religion too. ■

A DEATH IN THE FAMILY
6/4/63

19. Hot Spots

WEATHERWISE—if that's the word—all I know aside from what I get on the broadcasts is what I hear on the telephone when I dial that number. And this information is generally delivered in a voice that has on me a numbing, hypnotic effect which results in my listening to the recording three times around, nodding, hanging up, and remembering nothing for sure except "Thankyew for cawling."

Many of the TV forecasts, on the other hand, give me the weather in a way that I manage to grasp more easily, if I can manage to get through them. They don't just tell me what the weather is and what we can expect later. They start way out there where the weather begins and practically tell me how the comet got its tail and how the cirrocumulus cloud got its stripes. They take the weather all across the continent—west to east, and north to south; and if they start any further north, they are literally going to fulfill the little boy's complaint about the book that "tells me more about penguins than I want to know." They tell me about cold fronts and warm fronts and air masses and give me a rundown on what it's like all over the country, just in case I should want to make a quick nonstop tour, or should be wondering if Aunt Effie can make it to the mailbox in Missoula.

By the time they close in on my city (which is generally just when the phone rings), I am all agog and alert. It looks as if we're going to have nice weather with no noticeable precipitation, and gentle northerly winds—altogether a delightful day—unless, that is, this mass of cool air with the diagonal lines here should move down *here,* and this warm front with the crosshatch lines should bypass that area and take a right turn at the next corner. In *that* case, of course, all bets are off.

I'm not in the predicting business and glad of it, because I don't envy those fellows. But in a runthrough of the international scene, it's a safe bet that there will continue to be hot spots, many of them in hot places, such as the Congo and Southeast Asia, and with no clear charts on the origin or duration of the heat.

The cold front of the Berlin wall still faces Berliners—with the climate there periodically hot, cold and temperate. And the UN quarters in New York have frequently been one of the hottest spots of all.

Temperatures in Washington and Moscow have been generally more moderate. Of course, if there should be unusual turbulence or east-west high-pressure areas, a cold war front could move back again. Happily, there has been a noticeable drop in fallout. However, if more little mushroom-shaped clouds should originate in the West in French territory, and if others should start coming up in the East from China . . . ■

"OUT OF THIS NETTLE, DANGER, WE PLUCK THIS FLOWER, SAFETY."
7/22/59

"HE ASKED, 'HOW ABOUT A FREE COUNTRY?' "
12/14/58

"STOP FLOWING, DO YOU HEAR?"
8/10/61

THE BUILDERS
8/27/61

8/11/63

"THOSE CRAZY BUDDHISTS— SETTING FIRE TO THEMSELVES."

8/30/63

"AND SO'S MY OLD MAN!"

10/17/63

11/4/63

"OKAY, BOY—WE'LL LET YOU CO-EXIST WITH US A WHILE LONGER."

11/18/60

"ANYONE ELSE WHO DOESN'T BELIEVE IN THE ABOMINABLE SNOWMAN?"

10/31/62

"WHO DO YOU THINK YOU ARE—INDONESIANS?"

9/20/63

"I WAS JUST TELLING KHRUSHCHEV, 'OUR DIFFERENCES ARE ONLY TEMPORARY.'"

4/18/64

"AND HERE IS LAOS, WE HOPE–"
6/15/62

PLAIN OF JARS
5/27/64

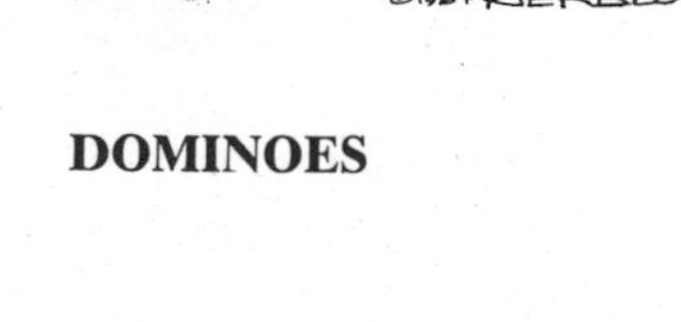

DOMINOES
5/24/64

"BASICALLY THERE ARE THREE GOVERNMENTS INVOLVED–THE DIEM GOVERNMENT, THE U.S.A. AND THE C.I.A."
9/10/63

"YOU KNOW, I DON'T THINK THE U.N. EVER REPLIED TO OUR ULTIMATUM LAST YEAR."
4/23/59

"WHICH DID YOU SAY ARE THE NEW NATIONS?"
9/30/60

"YOU'RE GOING TO HAVE TO BE A BIG MAN NOW."
9/21/61

"DON'T RIGHTLY KNOW IF I CAN SPARE A NAIL."
8/3/62

"BUT I GAVE HIM HIS INDEPENDENCE, DIDN'T I?"

7/22/60

UP FROM THE JUNGLE

8/5/60

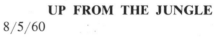

"WE MUST JOIN TO AVENGE OUR DEAR FRIEND, LUMUMBA."

2/16/61

1/11/63

20. Code of the Hill

"PAPA, what is ethics?" asks the little boy in the old story.

"I'll give you an example," replies the father. "Suppose a man walks into my store, buys a tube of toothpaste, and hands me a bill. I give him the change from a dollar bill and he leaves. But just as he is going out the door, I notice that what he gave me was actually a twenty-dollar bill. Now, here is where *ethics* comes in. The question is 'Should I tell my partner?' "

Off and on over a period of years, Congress, which has scrutinized conflicts of interest in other parts of the government, has considered the matter of its own ethics. And in the 1963-64 session, members of the U.S. Senate gave serious thought to what they should tell their legislative partners and the country at large about their own finances.

The immediate cause of the Senate soul-searching was the case of Bobby Baker, former secretary to the Senate Majority, and a young man who had acquired unusual influence and affluence.

In September 1963, the Washington *Post* disclosed that Mr. Baker had an interest in a vending machine company that did most of its business in defense plants. This set off an inquiry into other Baker affairs, which included an interest in a plush motel, real estate deals, a travel agency, interesting stock transactions, and a government "disaster loan." There was also a Baker town house with lavender wall-to-wall carpeting, which was actually occupied by two girls—one a former Baker employee, the other a former employee of Senator George Smathers of Florida.

Mr. Baker's Senate connections apparently did him no harm in his business enterprises and

"DOWN, BOY—NOT THAT ONE—
DOWN, YOU DUMB MUTT."

10/13/63

"YOU MAY QUESTION THE SERVANTS ONLY. AFTER ALL, THIS IS A GENTLEMEN'S CLUB."
5/15/64

speculative activities, one of which involved Senator Smathers, who explained that he and Mr. Baker happened to do a little investing that fortunately turned out to be successful. But Mr. Baker's connections were not limited to one or two legislators. And there was a fine nonpartisanship about his activities, which involved also Republican Congressman John W. Byrnes of Wisconsin, who interceded with the Treasury Department in behalf of a Milwaukee insurance company in which he and Mr. Baker had purchased stock at special low prices.

It was often commented upon that Mr. Baker, who had come to Washington as a Senate page, was actually "a child of the Senate." So attention turned to the senatorial environment which had influenced the young man who learned to influence people enough to build up a little empire of outside financial interest valued on paper at more than $2,000,000.

The Bobby Baker case was complete with stories about lavish entertaining and call girls.

Less newsy but probably more important than how he lined his pockets was the reported Baker claim that he had ten senators in his pocket; and less juicy but more important than stories of call girls was his influence upon roll calls in the Senate. Here the highly knowledgeable Mr. Baker's oddly inaccurate estimates on some key votes reportedly were involved in the narrow defeat of Kennedy Administration bills.

Several liberal senators charged that Baker had lied in his dealings with them, and that by misrepresenting their statements and their wishes on committee assignments he had kept them from committee positions to which they were entitled.

The Baker investigation, which even involved the juggling of Senate page salaries, spurred a demand for disclosures of business activities and outside incomes not only of Senate employees but of senators themselves.

As far back as 1951, President Truman had called for a law to require all government employees (including congressmen and military men) who received more than $10,000 a year to make public financial statements annually. Several senators and representatives of that period

"FORTUNATELY, THE TRANSACTION DID TURN OUT SUCCESSFULLY."
1/15/64

"I DECLARE, I DON'T KNOW WHERE-ALL THE LAD PICKED UP SUCH HABITS."
11/19/63

expressed solemn concern over a mink coat or a deep freeze, but Mr. Truman's "public-office-is-a-privilege" proposal didn't seem to interest them.

Among the first senators to make voluntary disclosures of their incomes were Stephen Young (D-Ohio), Wayne Morse (D-Ore.) and Clifford Case (R-N.J.). Other senators listed as having done likewise by early 1964 were Joseph Clark (D-Pa.), Jacob Javits (R-N.Y.), Kenneth Keating (R-N.Y.), Hugh Scott (R-Pa.), William Proxmire (D-Wis.) and Paul Douglas (D-Ill.).

The strongest of the resolutions proposed in the Senate in 1964 would have required senators and Senate employees to list sources of income in excess of $10,000 a year.

On July 27, 1964, this was voted down 48 to 39, after an impassioned plea by Senator Everett Dirksen, who gave an oration on the honor and dignity of the Senate, which he apparently felt was upheld by refraining from financial disclosures. The Senate instead preferred to consider a Dirksen proposal to create a commission that would study and deliberate for two years on ethical standards in all branches of the government. It was once said of a politician that he wrestled with his conscience and lost. Perhaps the same could be said of the U.S. Senate.

The honor and dignity of lawmakers have been upheld in about the same curious way by failure to reform laws on campaign contributions. For some reason, Congress has not adopted recommendations to broaden the base of contributions and keep public officials from being unduly indebted to large contributors.

In 1962 there had been much interest in the financial empire of Billy Sol Estes, who had also built up a fortune, based partly on the sale or leasing of nonexistent fertilizer tanks.

But Kennedy Administration proposals for revisions of farm programs and of tax laws to prevent future manipulations aroused somewhat less enthusiasm than the Estes case itself.

Large contributions from oil companies have also failed to arouse the indignation of many lawmakers—especially those lawmakers on the receiving end of the contributions.

"CAREFUL, NOW."
12/18/63

ENGRAVE IT IN LETTERS OF GOLD
1/16/64

"NEW PIECES KEEP TURNING UP."
1/31/64

"AND SO, THE CURTAIN FALLS— I SAID, '*AND SO, THE CURTAIN FALLS!*'"
3/19/64

GROWS LIKE MAGIC
5/16/62

In an old Amos-and-Andy program, a unique explanation of banking finance is given to a simple character who had deposited money in a savings account. On trying to make a withdrawal, he is told that he *did* have money in his account, but the interest "et up the principal." The principles of some legislators seem to get et up by their private interests.

Congress has been more interested in the finances of others than in disclosures concerning its own finances; but it has not always been relentless in pursuing financial matters involving other parts of the government either.

Both in Congress and in the press there was probably more attention focused on Sherman Adams' carpet than on all the other gifts to members of the Eisenhower Administration—including the amazing number of highly valuable nonofficial gifts showered on President Eisenhower himself. To that much-gifted President a deep-freeze or a hi-fi set would have been items of no consequence—as, in fact, they were of no real consequence to other Presidents, though they were much publicized.

Senator Stuart Symington's Armed Services Subcommittee went after really big game in its investigations of government stockpiling deals, which were "military secrets" for many years till President Kennedy opened them for investigation early in his administration. Mr. Kennedy said at a news conference in January 1962 that there was evidence of "excessive and unconscionable profits" in the government stockpile program.

Hundreds of millions of dollars were involved in purchases which included supplies far in excess of anything that could possibly be needed, and goods unloaded upon the government because they could not be sold elsewhere.

Commentator Edward P. Morgan, reporting on some of the stockpile scandals, told of testimony that one company "sold to the United States over a period of nine years, 900,000 tons of uncommonly low-grade ore for a net profit of $4,226,177.03 on a $238,000 investment,

"NOW ARE YOU READY TO REPAIR THE HENHOUSE?"
5/18/62

STOCKPILE

2/1/63

"—IN ARRIVING AT THIS DECISION—"
9/23/58

"THAT HOUND IS HOWLING AGAIN."
3/27/60

"LET'S PUT IT THIS WAY—THE LAST ADMINISTRATION ACHIEVED A SCIENTIFIC BREAKTHROUGH IN ALCHEMY."
6/24/62

"LET'S SAY IT WASN'T EXACTLY A 'TIGHT MONEY' POLICY."
8/17/62

only $19,000 of which, reportedly, was cash."

Enormous quantities of castor oil and feathers were among the stockpile items; but some of the largest profits were apparently made on minerals.

Senator Henry Dworshak (R-Idaho) disclosed on July 18, 1962, that former President Eisenhower himself suggested helping the distressed mining industry by buying lead and zinc for the national stockpile. And Senator Symington declared that the multimillion-dollar lead-zinc purchases were made through illegal actions by government officials who had no authority to use the stockpile program to sustain or boost prices.

A UPI story in April 1962 reported:

> Two Eisenhower Administration Cabinet members set up a procedure under which copper-mining companies reaped "windfall" profits of nearly $3 million at government expense, Senate investigators were told yesterday.
>
> A witness for the General Services Administration identified the men as former Treasury Secretary George M. Humphrey and former Commerce Secretary Sinclair Weeks....

George M. Humphrey had apparently been quite a salesman, being involved also in sales of nickel to the government. And probably no one was more successful than he in selling political policies to President Eisenhower. Indeed, in 1964 Mr. Humphrey was credited with selling General Eisenhower a Goldwater button—or at least unselling him on a Scranton one.

Mr. Humphrey and his M. A. Hanna companies were listed high among those accused of making unconscionable profits and of misrepresenting costs. Mr. Humphrey was additionally accused of having retained his interests in the Hanna Company while serving in the government.

Mr. Humphrey seemed to have not only plenty of copper and nickel but even more brass. And at Senate hearings he lectured and shouted at the committee. People with less money and with better causes have not always done so well before Congressional committees. And despite Senator Symington's heated exchanges with Mr. Humphrey, the committee did not pursue the Hanna interests and Mr.

THE AGE OF PYRAMID BUILDING
12/12/62

Humphrey by boring in on them. Mr. Humphrey was left with all his gold and all his brass intact.

Probably the most quoted lines in Sherman Adams' book, *Firsthand Report,* have been those which came toward the end, when he mentioned a conversation between President Eisenhower and Treasury Secretary George Humphrey:

> Eisenhower asked him if it were not possible for American businessmen to make some sacrifices . . . in the interests of world peace.
>
> "No," Humphrey said candidly. "The American businessman believes in getting as much as he can while the getting is good."
>
> "Maybe that's the trouble with businessmen, George," Eisenhower said seriously.

If that was not the trouble with businessmen, perhaps it was, at least, the trouble with George —and with letting George do it.

Hundreds of millions of dollars of government funds were involved in sales of nickel, lead, zinc and other minerals. But cases like this did not stir the same general interest that others have. Perhaps they lacked sex appeal. No motels, no girls in town houses, or lavender wall-to-wall carpeting—just plain wall-to-wall money. ■

"NOW, ABOUT CONFLICTS OF INTEREST–UH, LET'S SEE, WHERE WAS I?"

3/16/61

"WHAT ARE YOU, SOME KIND OF A FRESH AIR NUT?"

4/25/62

"ON YOUR TOES, NOW! I WANT ALL OF YOU CLEAN AND FIT."

10/7/62

"OH, ANTI-NEGRO, EH?"

2/22/63

21. Rich Man, Poor Man...

A LOT OF people have a fine philosophical and spiritual attitude toward poverty. And at the drop of a hungry man, they can recite: *The poor ye have with you always* and *God helps those who help themselves*. This is a great comfort to them and spares them a lot of worry.

Government policy in recent years has been less pious, more helpful and more realistic. It has recognized the existence of poverty in other countries; and, through foreign aid programs, has tried to alleviate the sufferings of people abroad. More than that, it has faced the fact of continuing poverty in the United States and has recognized the government's obligation to do something about it.

The poor today may not be as much in evidence or in such sharp contrast as they were in days when beggars held out their caps to gentlemen in silk hats—but they get just as hungry. And those people who can't see poverty can read about it in their papers, in reports from news writers, from government agencies, and from pollsters.

In June 1964, *Newsweek* summarized a Louis Harris poll which compared the concerns of Americans 30 years ago with those of today. The poll showed that today one family in six has one mentally ill member; one family in five has the hopeless problem of the elderly dependent or one member incurably ill.

"In contrast," the *Newsweek* report continued, "the survey shows only 14 per cent of adults without enough to eat . . ."

The contrast is with the days when President Roosevelt saw one-third of a nation "ill-housed, ill-clad, ill-nourished." But the *only 14 per cent without enough to eat*—in the United States in prosperous 1964—is still shocking.

Such figures, along with news stories of Americans going hungry in Appalachia and in metropolitan areas in the North, underscore a need for welfare and anti-poverty programs that may not always be apparent on a drive from a comfortable suburban home to the office and back.

Even less apparent to most Americans is the

"I WANT TO SAVE YOU FROM INFLATION AND EXTRAVAGANCE."
7/8/59

WALL-TO-WALL UNDER-THE-CARPETING
7/18/63

"THEY'VE BEEN GOING TOGETHER FOR QUITE A WHILE."

11/19/61

kind of condition which W. M. Newman of the Chicago Daily News Service reported from Mississippi. There, he said, "Negroes live worse, eat worse, and die faster" and their "median yearly income for individual workers was an unbelievably low $724, according to the U.S. Census. That meant that half of the state's Negroes were earning under that figure and half over."

It has been an interesting switch on traditional political behavior that the party in office during the election year of 1964 was most outspoken about such conditions.

In August 1964, when the Labor Department reported a new all-time employment high and an unemployment drop to below 5 per cent, Secretary of Labor Willard W. Wirtz called these figures "encouraging" but continued to insist that we could not be satisfied till full employment was reached. And while President Johnson was obviously pleased to report economic gains, he kept plugging for his antipoverty program, which Congress passed the same month.

Hard-line Goldwaterites, on the other hand, followed their leader in his feeling about the poor and unemployed: that "most people who have no skill, have no education for the same reason—low intelligence or low ambition"; and his opinion that there should be an examination of "the attitude" of those "not participating in the general prosperity."

You there—you with the hungry look. What's the matter you're not *participating?* You trying to make us look bad? You un-American or something?

Of all the well-to-do men to become prominent in politics, Senator Goldwater has distinguished himself by being consistently the champion of the overdog. And while others were interested in civil rights, the Senator displayed toward those less fortunate than himself an uncivil righteousness.

In Newburgh, New York, in July 1961, City Manager Joseph Mitchell put through a stringent 13-point "welfare code" designed to restrict tightly payments to people on relief, and to crack down on relief "chiselers."

"WE HAVE DISCOVERED A PARTICULARLY DANGEROUS PIECE OF RADICAL, SUBVERSIVE PROPAGANDA."

4/14/63

Some of the features of this get-tough code were the cutting off of relief to families after three months of aid in any given year; the denying of relief to unwed mothers if additional children were born out of wedlock after the family qualified for relief; a requirement that able-bodied males work 40 hours a week for their relief checks; and a limit of one or two weeks' aid to newcomers.

Senator Goldwater wrote a letter to Mitchell expressing admiration for him, visited with Mitchell on July 18, and said, as reported in a UPI story on the front page of *The New York Times* the following day, "I don't like to see my taxes paid for children born out of wedlock"; "I'm tired of professional chiselers walking up and down the streets who don't work and have no intention of working. I would like to see every city in the country adopt the [Newburgh] plan"—which he endorsed in its entirety and about which he said he had no reservations.

As Eve Edstrom later reported in the Washington *Post*, all welfare recipients who were able to walk were required to turn out at police stations, in order that fraud might be disclosed; but not one case of fraud was discovered. And

ROSE GARDEN

4/26/64

"HE'S ALSO TURNED *ON* SOME LIGHTS."

4/30/64

an investigation by New York State officials revealed that one man, a white unemployed steelworker and a native of Newburgh, was considered able to work. But he was excused when he reported for duty, because his wife was in the hospital and there was no one to care for their five children. "This able-bodied man, incidentally, has one eye," Mrs. Edstrom disclosed.

Incidentally, also, on August 5, Mr. Mitchell disclosed that he was introducing what he described as "thought control" to see that case workers were in "philosophical harmony" with the city administration's ideas on government.

The Newburgh "welfare" program proved not only to be unduly harsh and unrealistic, but was also found, in August 1961, to be illegal; and Newburgh was enjoined from enforcing 12 points of its 13-point code.

When Mr. Mitchell resigned his position in Newburgh he announced that he was accepting an organizational position with the John Birch Society. He later decided against the Birch job, but with no hard feelings. "I'm a moderate," he said in a 1963 statement. "The moderates are in the John Birch Society. The extremists are running the Federal government." In July 1964, Mr. Mitchell turned up in the news again, this time as a field director for the segregationist Citizens' Councils of America.

As for Senator Goldwater, he doesn't seem to spend any time looking back at what others might consider errors. He shows the same agility as did his old colleague, the late Senator Joe McCarthy—whose work he admired and whom he consistently supported—in leaping from one untenable position to another. At a meeting of Republicans in Atlanta, in November of the "Newburgh plan" year, he said, "I would like to see our party back up on school integration. The Supreme Court decision is not the supreme law of the land."

Shortly afterward, in an article datelined Phoenix, Arizona, which was published on December 3, Relman Morin of the Associated Press gave some interesting Goldwater quotes, including this one: "Except for Harry Truman, who wasn't very good at it, none of our Presidents in recent years was a man who ever had to meet a payroll." The others were, of course, President Roosevelt, President Eisenhower and President Kennedy.

On December 5, I drew the "If You Had Any Initiative..." cartoon, which was published the following day.

It was reprinted, accompanied in each case by a characteristic explanatory comment, in both *Time* Magazine and *Pravda,* two publications that I regard as being of equal reliability. *Pravda* neglected to identify the Senator and gave the impression that this was a typical American well-to-do or wealthy man.

The article in *Time,* the "newsmagazine"—which one newspaper columnist has referred to, in charitable understatement, as the house organ of the Republican party—is reprinted here:

> **Low Blow**
>
> The forceful—and liberal—brush of the Washington *Post's* editorial cartoonist Herbert L. Block is ever at the ready to assault Herblock's favorite target: the conservative. Artistic discipline generally keeps his passionate partiality within decent bounds (although he once showed former Vice President Richard M. Nixon crawling out of a sewer). But last week, as he sighted in on conservative U.S. Senator (and heir to Phoenix's Goldwaters department store) Barry M. Goldwater, nothing held Herblock back. He got off one of the lowest blows in his editorial-cartooning career *(see cut).*

That's the complete item. No Goldwater statements on the poor, on relief "chiselers," the Newburgh code, Mitchell, segregation of schoolchildren, or the crack at President Kennedy and his predecessors; nothing like that—just another "assault" on "conservatives."

The caveman "conservative" policies toward welfare recipients, toward unmarried mothers on relief—as well as get-tough policies toward others in trouble—are, by no coincidence, proposed by the same upstanding citizens who are least interested in meeting the needs or improving the environment of these people.

Of course, these "good, successful people" who chastise the less fortunate are not mean or heartless. As some of Senator Goldwater's admirers told me, Goodness gracious, the Senator wouldn't want to hurt those *children* born out of wedlock. Of course not. But he didn't explain what was to become of those children after the crackdown on their mothers. If the children were to be taken away and raised in groups, wouldn't that be socialistic or communistic or something? Also, apart from humane reasons for not yanking children away from mothers

"IF YOU HAD ANY INITIATIVE, YOU'D GO OUT AND INHERIT A DEPARTMENT STORE."

12/6/61

"LOOK—THINGS ARE PICKING UP."
3/3/59

"I'VE GOT THE HAPPY-DAYS-ARE-HERE-AGAIN BLUES."
6/28/61

"IF YOU DON'T MIND DANGER, YOU CAN SERVE IN ONE OF OUR CITIES AT HOME."
11/23/62

"THAT'S RIGHT, CHIEF—WE'RE LOOKING THIS ONE STRAIGHT IN THE EYE, BUT HE'S NOT BLINKING."
4/2/63

and institutionalizing them, there's no reason to think that this solution would save the taxpayer money, anyhow. As for the effect on the mothers themselves, there hasn't been much evidence that poverty contributes to family planning. Indeed, as Mrs. Edstrom pointed out in one of her articles, the illegitimate child is often a "grocery bag baby"–the result of an illicit relationship entered into to meet immediate food needs without regard for what may happen nine months later.

Even greater than the concern of righteous people about sin is the general concern over the increase in crime and juvenile delinquency. But the policies proposed often seem no more effective than those employed by the people of Samuel Butler's *Erewhon,* who put the sick in jail for being sick.

It is not "coddling" to try to insure that all Americans get a fair chance in life, and to see that all shall be protected in their legal rights. And it may be that the term "coddled" has been applied to the wrong group.

The crime waves don't seem to be stemmed by the advocates of nothing but tougher and tougher punishment for the boys and girls. Perhaps we should develop a get-tough policy toward the bigger boys–the bigger boys of wealth and power in politics, who set the time bombs of poverty and squalor, of ignorance and mental illness, which later explode in the street crimes that wake us up.

The people who would withhold aid and understanding from others are always finer and more noble and of better "moral fiber" than the less fortunate who get into jams. They are never just plain luckier to have been born in the right environment, at the right time, with the right IQ's, and even the right color skin. To support their views–and incidentally to suggest their own virtue–they will point out that many people of humble beginnings (often including their own modest little old selves) have been able to make good. And they can cite cases of people born in well-to-do or rich families who have committed crimes. This is supposed to explain everything, and to prove that anybody can be good, clever, and successful, if he will just stop being determined to be ignorant, poor, stupid, lazy and just plain bad.

They could as easily point to any white man on Skid Row and then cite the distinguished statesman and Nobel Prize winner Dr. Ralph Bunche as proof that skin coloration has never had anything to do with opportunities in our country.

As the late Franklin P. Adams observed, "The race is not to the swift, nor the battle to the strong; but the betting is best that way." The names that keep turning up on the police blotters are not *always* those of the indigent and the ignorant or the indigent-ignorant "repeaters"–but the statistics show that it would be foolish to gamble on any higher-educated or higher-economic-level groups coming in at the police stations and jails any more than a remote second.

One reason that many of the poor gravitate toward jails has been their inability to afford legal defense, and ignorance of their rights before the law, a condition the Supreme Court recognized in its decisions on the right of everyone to counsel. It was on the subject of bail that Attorney General Robert F. Kennedy spoke in 1964, when he said, "We can see to it that America does not unjustly punish the man who is already serving a life sentence of poverty. . . ."

But such matters have not been of interest to the comfortably righteous who sound like holdovers from the days of Charles Dickens.

Programs to fight poverty and inequalities, here and abroad, are–if only a beginning–a

"YOU KNOW WHAT? THOSE GUYS ACT LIKE THEY REALLY BELIEVE THAT."

3/21/63

recognition of basic cause and effect and of humane considerations. Conscience calls for such programs and self-interest demands them.

As President Kennedy pointed out, the percentage of our national income spent for foreign aid can hardly be regarded as a great sacrifice to us or as a burden that we should find tiring.

The cost of all the economic and welfare programs is less than that of crime and unemployment, and a bare fraction of the cost of arms and wars—in which "toughness" is carried to the limit.

We shake our heads with amazement when we read that Haitian dictator "Papa Doc" Duvalier practices voodoo; and there are few who believe any more that those afflicted with epilepsy and mental illness are possessed by evil spirits.

We might now advance to the point where we no longer regard the poor, the criminal —or the hungry man abroad who is tempted to bow down before strange ideologies—as possessed by evil spirits either. We can at least recognize that a little additional expenditure of effort and money can provide a more effective magic than pious mumbo-jumbo chants and spear-waving get-tough rites. ■

TRIBAL RITUAL

8/22/63

"—AND HIS FATHER LIVES UP THERE."

2/11/62

"NO MORE MAÑANA, SEÑOR."
3/15/61

WORLD-WIDE NON-MISSILE GAP
2/23/61

"PARA EL PROGRESO, SÍ! ALREADY I'VE WRITTEN TO WASHINGTON FOR FOLDERS ON THE NEW MODELS."
8/12/62

"MY, YOU GAVE ME A START! AT FIRST I THOUGHT YOU HAD A BEARD AND A CIGAR."
5/29/63

THE UNDER-THE-BEDSIDE MANNER
6/16/60

"SIR, SEVERAL MORE OF OUR MEN HAVE DEFECTED TO THE ENEMY."
1/10/61

"OPEN WIDE AND SAY 'BAH.'"
2/26/61

"I THINK HE SHOULD HAVE A CHOICE OF DOCTORS."
3/28/62

"JUDGE, I'D LIKE A SEPARATION."
6/25/59

"YES SIR—WE HAVE TO KEEP HUNTING WASTE IN THOSE FOREIGN AID PROGRAMS."
6/7/60

"GENTLEMEN, WE MAY NEED TO GIVE UP OUR LIVES—OR, EVEN WORSE, A FEW EXTRA DOLLARS."
9/14/61

"WE ARE DETERMINED TO FIGHT COMMUNISM BY ANY MEANS SHORT OF ACTUAL SPENDING."
9/19/62

22. The March

AUGUST 28, 1963, was the day of the March on Washington for Jobs and Freedom. As Negroes and whites gathered from around the nation, there was apprehension that some racists might touch off a disturbance; that with the capital filled with crowds arriving almost all on one day, all kinds of difficulties might ensue.

A few of us went early to the Lincoln Memorial, to which the marchers would come after gathering at the Washington Monument at about ten o'clock. The great wooden stands set up in front of the Lincoln Memorial were empty save for the ushers. It was a hot day and the sun was already warming the long empty rows of benches.

A few more entered the unfilled stands. One of the men in our group went to the nearby press tent and brought back some Cokes. Behind our sunglasses we squinted down toward the Washington Monument and saw nothing but the long reflecting pool and the trees. And then there was another unhappy thought, though not so awful as the possibility of disorders. Suppose the whole much-discussed march was a fizzle? After all, no one could estimate the numbers who would be arriving for

POPLARVILLE, MISSISSIPPI, U.S.A., 1959

4/28/59

JACKSON, MISS., MAY 25 . . . Gov. J. P. Coleman said he will make the FBI information available to the next regular session of the Grand Jury in November . . .

5/26/59

THE TIME HAS COME
FOR THIS NATION TO
FULFILL ITS PROMISES
©1963 HERBLOCK
THE WASHINGTON POST

WASHINGTON, D.C., JUNE 1963

6/13/63

this one day—by bus, by car, on foot, by bicycle, by whatever means. There was no way of calculating what this gathering would be like.

Finally, around noon, they began to come. From the streets behind the trees that bordered the bright reflecting pool, they came around both sides to the Memorial. The stands began to fill rapidly. They kept coming, Negro and white, old and young—not marching in the literal sense, of course, and not marching *on* anything, but *to* something. They found places to sit down in front of the Lincoln Memorial until the stands were full.

And they *kept* coming. After they filled the stands, they filled the street in front and the circle around; they filled the park area all about the Lincoln Memorial. They came—more than 200,000 people. Never in such a vast, hot crowd had everyone been so kind, courteous and friendly. I think everyone there felt proud, glad that he was a part of this occasion.

There was singing for about an hour till the formal program began. There were representatives of all the leading Negro organizations, of the churches, the labor unions, civic groups, fraternal orders, and the Government in the attendance of 150 members of Congress. There were Dr. Ralph Bunche and Walter Reuther; there were Marian Anderson and Mahalia Jackson and many movie stars and entertainers. There was Roy Wilkins, and Whitney M. Young, Jr., and the Reverend Fred Shuttlesworth. There was the father of the march, A. Philip Randolph, who had long dreamed of such a day. And then there was the Reverend Dr. Martin Luther King, Jr., who also had a dream. Over and over again, he said, "I have a dream . . ." It was the American dream, and we were a part of it.

Bayard Rustin read a statement of the marchers' goals. And the great crowd called back "Yes!" and "Pass the bill!" To the reading of a pledge to continue fighting for civil rights back home, the marchers cried a responsive "I do pledge."

"Then," reported Susanna McBee in the

Washington *Post,* "the throng, which Josephine Baker had called a 'salt and pepper crowd,' began singing 'We shall overcome.' Many of the people lining the reflecting pool in a magnificent picture-postcard setting, held hands and swayed back and forth as they sang. Then they dispersed and it was all over."

The March itself was a success beyond a dream. No disturbance anywhere marred that bright day.

The conduct and dignity of the marchers were noted by the government, by the nation, by the world.

Almost twenty-five years before, Marian Anderson had sung from the steps before that same figure of Abraham Lincoln. A march had been going on all that time, and I had seen eighteen years of it since I came to Washington after the war—to a capital in which theaters, hotels, restaurants and schools were still segregated.

In Washington, desegregation began in restaurants, following a Supreme Court case which came the year before the famous 1954 school decision. Washington is largely a Southern city, and at each step of the way there were forebodings about the spread of desegregation. When theaters were picketed, there were fears that if they were desegregated—well, you might have heaven knows what. They were desegregated—slowly and quietly — and nothing happened. Most people didn't even know exactly when the change occurred. If anyone ever walked out of a theater or failed to attend as a result of the change, I never heard about it. And it was the same with other integration moves.

The cartoon of the restaurant and the dark-skinned couple from abroad was based on something that actually happened in a Washington restaurant years before. A nervous tearoom hostess eyed a pair of Negro girls who stood in the line waiting for tables.

As others were seated and the two girls came toward the front of the line, she grew more apprehensive. Finally, when they were close enough, she overheard them speaking to each

THE WHITE MAN'S BURDEN
3/26/59

"YOU THINK HE MIGHT GET INTERESTED IN US IF WE MOVED TO SOUTH AFRICA?"
4/5/60

"IT'S ALL RIGHT TO SEAT THEM. THEY'RE NOT AMERICANS."

4/27/61

other in French; with great relief she whispered to her assistant that it would be all right to seat them—they were French.

But years later it required a special appeal from the U.S. government to some restaurateurs in Maryland and Virginia to please avoid embarrassing the nation by refusing to seat foreign diplomats who were non-white. And some grudgingly agreed that they would seat dark-skinned foreign diplomats—but not Americans.

When Washington schools were integrated, some segregationist papers sent men to the capital to watch like vultures for violence—and when no serious trouble occurred, they reported desegregation a failure anyhow. Of course, there had to be some period of adjustment when Negro children, educated in clearly inferior "separate but equal" schools, required additional training. This was due not to the cure, integration, but to the cause, previous years of neglect.

And then there was also the man with the movie camera, from somewhere outside the capital, who had come to take pictures of desegregated schools and had urged a little white boy to throw stones at a little colored boy to provide some "action." The white and Negro boys, being friends, and having more sense than the man with the movie camera, did not oblige.

There were, and still are, in the capital, some white cab drivers who will spout racist poison at you as they drive till you tell them to shut up or pull over to the curb and let you out.

But the march goes on, here and throughout the nation. It goes slowly sometimes, in some places, and there is resistance in a Deep North as well as a Deep South. There have been ugly

"WE'LL SEE HOW TOUGH THE NEW COP IS."

3/14/61

"OH, *'RIOTERS'*—AT FIRST I THOUGHT YOU SAID *'RIDERS'*! GO AHEAD."

5/18/61

"WE DON'T WANT NO TROUBLEMAKERS FROM THE UNITED STATES."

5/23/61

"IF THEAH'S ANYTHIN' AH LIKE, IT'S A GOOD JOKE."

4/24/62

"AND ANOTHER THING–"

5/4/62

"WHAT'S THE MATTER? WE DON'T SAY 'NIGGERS' UP HERE."

3/12/63

and brutal attacks, clubbings, murders, riots; the snarls of police dogs; and worse, the snarls of humans; and there will be more. There have also arisen some demagogues among Negroes, as well as the many among whites; and as new gains are made, there will be more who will seek to wrest control from responsible leaders. There will continue to be bigots and terrorists who will make it difficult for Negroes to remain patient and non-violent. There will be other cops like the one who surveyed a bombed Negro house and grinned as he said it looked to him "like termites" had done it.

There will be many people, white and black, acting through ignorance–and not surprisingly, since they were raised in ignorance. There are many for whom the march is too fast and many for whom it is too slow. But it goes on.

Throughout the dragging weeks and months of the 1964 Senate filibuster the march went on, with troubles and strife – and also with the infinite dignity and restraint that had characterized the Negro movement under responsible leaders, the dignity and restraint that had driven bigots to madness.

Through bloody rioting in Florida it went on, while Senator Smathers offered to pay the travel expenses of "outsiders" if they would leave the state. Many of us would gladly pay the travel expenses of a George Smathers and provide him with a one-way luxury-class ticket to any country of his choice–perhaps some dictatorship like the Dominican Republic, for which he showed so much sympathy. Ten years earlier Senator James Eastland said the choice between segregation and desegregation was the

ECLIPSE

5/31/63

"ASK THE UN-AMERICAN ACTIVITIES COMMITEE TO INVESTIGATE WHAT THIS STRANGE FLAG IS DOING DOWN HERE."

5/17/63

"THOSE ALABAMA STORIES ARE SICKENING.
WHY CAN'T THEY BE LIKE US AND FIND SOME NICE,
REFINED WAY TO KEEP THE NEGROES OUT?"

5/19/63

"FASTER!...HERE IT TAKES ALL THE RUNNING *YOU* CAN DO TO KEEP IN THE SAME PLACE."
5/30/63

choice between victory or defeat—and the "death of Southern culture."

There has been a lot of marching since then—marching to voter registration desks and to the polls. And there will be more and more marching to the polls.

The filibuster continued and at last the cloture vote was taken. Senator Goldwater voted against cloture, saying that he did so to protect the interests of Arizona as a small state. But any kid who had taken high school civics could have told him that the composition of the U.S. Senate itself was designed to provide all the protection considered necessary for small states—even in the days when Federal government was a new idea. Any intelligent youngster, black or white, could have told him that small states were never intended to have the power to obstruct the entire United States.

Finally there came the vote on the Civil Rights bill itself, when the same Senator voted against it, partly because, he said, the bill bid fair to result in an "informer" psychology, with "neighbors spying upon neighbors," and to provide inducement for "those who would harass their fellow citizens for selfish and narrow purposes."

This was a strange argument to make against a rights bill. And it was all the stranger coming from one whose entire career in the U.S. Senate had been marked by a callous unconcern for civil liberties—who had fully supported the "informer" psychology and "those who would harass their fellow citizens for selfish and nar-

"SORRY, BUT YOU HAVE AN INCURABLE SKIN CONDITION."

7/4/63

"LE-GIS-LA-TION, IT SHALL NOT BE MOVED."

7/17/63

"IMAGINE TRYING TO TELL PEOPLE WHAT THEY CAN DO IN THEIR OWN PLACES OF BUSINESS!"

7/7/63

row purposes" during the worst abuses of the McCarthy era.

But the march went on, and the bill became law.

Fifty-five weeks earlier, President Kennedy had called upon Congress to pass a Civil Rights bill, saying:

> ...We are confronted primarily with a moral issue. It is as old as the Scriptures and is as clear as the American Constitution.
>
> The heart of the question is whether all Americans are to be afforded equal rights and equal opportunities, whether we are going to treat our fellow Americans as we want to be treated...

On July 2, 1964, President Johnson said, as he signed the document:

> ...The purpose of this law is simple. It does not restrict the freedom of any American so long as he respects the rights of others. It does not give special treatment to any citizen.
>
> It does say that those who are equal before God shall now also be equal in the polling booths, in the classrooms, in the factories, and in hotels, restaurants, movie theaters and other places that provide service to the public...

Conscious of his responsibility to the nation

...CONCEIVED IN LIBERTY AND DEDICATED TO THE PROPOSITION THAT ALL MEN ARE CREATED EQUAL...

8/27/63

"OF COURSE, I ABHOR VIOLENCE— HAVE A BOOK OF CAMPAIGN MATCHES, BUD."

9/18/63

"AND REMEMBER, NOTHING CAN BE ACCOMPLISHED BY TAKING TO THE STREETS."

9/6/63

"WOULD YOU REPEAT THAT, SIR? THE AFTERNOON BOMB EXPLOSION JARRED THE MICROPHONE A LITTLE."

9/26/63

"HALF STEP! HALF STEP! YOU KEEP MARCHING TOO FAST."

10/18/63

and to history, the President appealed earnestly for the understanding of all Americans, and said that "we have come now to a time of testing"—words that recalled those spoken during a war "testing whether this nation or any nation so conceived and so dedicated can long endure."

For a hundred years since then the march had gone on. It had gone on before the nation began, even before the slave ships came. It will go on through debate and appeals to reason, and during incitements of extremists and rabble rousers. There will undoubtedly be more troubles, more riots, more injury and agony and dying.

And after all this, it will still go on; because it is the march not alone of one race but of the human race.

The end of the march can be envisioned in words spoken by Dr. Neil V. Sullivan, of the Prince Edward County Free School Association, when he said that we must join together and truly become "not our brother's keeper but . . . our brother's brother." It can be seen afar in the dream of Martin Luther King at the March on Washington, as he looked toward the day when all people everywhere "will be able to join hands and sing in the words of that old Negro spiritual, 'Free at last! Free at last! Thank God almighty, we are free at last!' " ■

"AND, OVER HERE, THE ENEMY—PEOPLE."

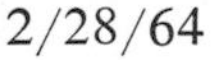
2/28/64

BROTHERHOOD

4/9/64

"SURE–I'M FOR EQUALIZING THINGS."
3/10/64

"WE'RE *ALL* READY FOR VOTING."
6/7/64

"WHO SAYS WE'RE NOT WILLING TO SIT DOWN TOGETHER?"
4/17/64

HANDWRITING ON THE WALL
5/31/64

"YOU DON'T UNDERSTAND, BOY—YOU'RE SUPPOSED TO JUST SHUFFLE ALONG."

5/15/63

23. Open for Postal Inspection

You should see the mail I get—particularly from magazines. I don't want to brag, but I've passed up some pretty special offers. They tell me what I've missed in the past few months, what I'm about to miss in the next few months, and what I will go right on missing. They include so many goodies that they are regular little souvenir stands in envelopes—pennies, stamps, buttons, imitation silver medallions, cutouts, puzzles, games, jumbo cards and folders, and telegram-type messages that open to the size of carpets. And letters with the signatures of publishers personally printed on them in blue ink.

Then there are the special offers that give me something to do with my hands. If I punch out of the big card the round cardboard button that says *YES*, and insert it into the little cardboard slot on the return card, and mail it in, they'll bill me for a subscription. And from another magazine there's a Special Offer Stamp, which, if I paste it in the blank square and mail it, will also get me billed as a subscriber. Good gravy, what if I were to get so excited and trembly that I missed the square? Maybe they'd give me a second chance. It might even be in the batch of offers that came in the next mail—which I haven't opened yet.

I don't mind telling you that I've also received from magazines some very official-looking certificates that look like bonds, and others that look like checks. I'm invited to initial and mail those back too, but I wouldn't want to take a chance on their going through the mail a second time; they belong in a safe-deposit box.

My special offers come in six more colors than the magazines themselves. I get from the same mazagine subscription offers for the Special Renewal rate, the Special Introductory rate, the Special New Friends rate, the Special Old Friends rate, the Special We've-Been-Missing-You rate—and for all I know they may have a Special Recently Departed rate, which comes right after the Special Lifetime rate.

Well, all these magazine solicitations are so ingenious and the flow is so constant that I don't have time to read the magazines themselves anymore. And if I did read them, I wouldn't subscribe to them without first checking through all the old piles of mail to see what

"STAND BACK—IT MAY BE A BOOK."
6/16/59

"SOME OF YOU STILL SEEM TO HAVE THE OLD-FASHIONED IDEA THAT WE'RE SUPPOSED TO DELIVER THE MAIL."

5/8/59

"BEAT IT! WHAT DO YOU THINK THIS IS—SOME KIND OF PUBLIC SERVICE OPERATION?"

5/20/64

their best offer was, or maybe even waiting to see what next week's closing quotation would be.

There was a time back in boyhood days when, for Papa's birthday, you gave him a subscription to the *Saturday Evening Post* or *Scientific American;* and when the subscription ran out a year later, or maybe two or three years later (I don't want you to think I was small about these things), you would renew it—taking care to get the renewal in before the issues stopped coming. It was the same with your own subscription to *St. Nicholas, Youth's Companion,* or *American Boy*. You were on what might today be called an annual cash basis. And save for a possible grace issue or two, when you stopped sending in money you stopped getting the magazine.

Today it is different. Expiration notices don't mean much any more; I even get them from publications that I never subscribed to in the first place. I am sure that all magazines and all other direct mail advertisers have a clearing house in which they swap mailing lists indiscriminately—the idea being to saturate every possible subscriber in the country with offers. Sometimes a magazine that is busily sending a fatter and faster flow of expiration notices, gets thinner and weaker, until finally *it* expires. But the subscription offers still continue with a life of their own—through other publications which have procured (and probably paid money for) the rights to this list of nonsubscribers. And like lemmings, these magazines follow each other into oblivion.

Magazine mailings and direct mail offers are things apart which run on continuously and independently. The renewal notices sometimes come with the first copy, and the magazines continue long after the expiration dates. Even the subscriber to a children's magazine must soon figure out that there is no sense taking the first offer if other and more enticing offers are to follow. The result is obvious:

The subscriber puts off renewing; the prospect puts off subscribing; and he certainly will not buy the magazine at the newsstand, because if there's one thing the magazine mailings have impressed on him, it's that anybody who pays full price for the magazine is a complete sap.

And with all the talent and effort and money going into direct mail campaigns, there isn't much left of the magazine anyhow. Pitted against the direct mail advertising, it finds itself outweighed and outmatched. It's no wonder the magazines worry about their second-class mailing rate; they might also worry about the bulk rate and any other rates for subscription offers. Some of their stuff is marked MAY BE OPENED FOR INSPECTION, and I'd suggest to the postal people that they don't bother, short-handed as they are already.

With all *that* stuff to be carted around, and all the "Occupant" mail and soap coupons, I can see that the Post Office Department must be kept pretty busy—even without congressmen trying to put through a law to allow them to flood their districts with Occupant mail of their own.

I sympathize with the clerks and carriers in particular. It must be pretty discouraging to my mailman to stuff a new wad of special offers and Occupant stuff into my mailbox and turn around to see the trash man carting off last week's batch.

I understand the problems of the mail; and I realize that there are certain annoyances the Post Office Department isn't really responsible for. Some are due to Congressional law—like provisions about asking recipients if they want to receive "foreign propaganda" mail. Some of it is according to Natural law—like the less important letters being the ones that are sent special delivery; and the least important ones being those for which you are wakened earliest.

"LET'S MOVE IT, BUSTER."
2/19/61

"GREETINGS, OCCUPANT."
3/2/60

But taking all those things into account, I still think the Post Office Department could do better.

During the Eisenhower Administration, Postmaster General Arthur Summerfield used to worry a lot about what we read, and tried to save us from dangerous books like *Lady Chatterley's Lover.* He didn't exactly replace the package-drop mailboxes with washing machines, but he was so deeply concerned that the literature we received should be clean, clean, clean, that some of us got a little concerned about him too.

Postmaster General J. Edward Day got the Postal Department out of the detergent field and back to the mail business. And then Mr. John Gronouski came along. *He* apparently read about lights being turned off in the White House, and figured that what was good enough there was good enough for the post offices.

In large metropolitan areas, where they used to be open day and night every day of the year, they began closing early and staying closed over weekends. And services like parcel post were curtailed. The new motto seemed to be that nothing was to stay those couriers from the swift depletion of their appointed rounds. And the ranks of the couriers themselves were depleted too, because another feature of this big economy drive was that as employees retired or resigned, a lot of them simply were not replaced.

Maybe it's just my imagination, but the service always seems to be cut just after the postage rate goes up; and every time the service is cut, we see a picture in the paper of some new post office gimmick. Under Mr. Summerfield it was a talking stamp machine that said nothing but a few clean words of thanks, and which was just what we didn't need and which we never heard from or heard of again. He also painted the mailboxes three colors instead of one, which must have been a great economy. And with a stroke of genius, he managed, in some busy locations, to place red-white-and-blue mailboxes right next to blue-white-and-red ones, so that you never can be sure which is for airmail.

When Mr. Gronouski got to chopping the service, there was a picture in the paper of a fluorescent mailbox. I don't know whether it was bright enough to read by, but apparently it was supposed to offer a little comforting light during the gloom of night that stayed the post offices from operating, while you waited till morning if you so much as wanted to buy a stamp from them. In July 1964, Postmaster General Gronouski relented to the extent of restoring part of the services he had cut.

The economy wave did not extend to knocking off the profit on sales of stamps from vending machines, which bring no additional revenue to the government, although they represent a markup of 25 per cent and more on the face value of stamps. One member of the House of Representatives was moved to inquire aloud in Congress about this price discrepancy. Robert L. Asher wrote, in the Washington *Post,* that the Congressman was tired of taking a licking on his stamps; and Mr. Asher went on to coin a nickel slogan with a right true ring: What this country needs is a good five-cent stamp for five cents—and on a 24-hour-a-day basis.

The Congressman proposed that vending machines owned and operated by Uncle Sam be placed next to every collection box and sell stamps at face value to match the honest faces that appear on them. The Post Office Department wondered about temperature changes and moisture problems, fearing that the snow, rain, and heat which didn't stop the couriers might possibly slow up the stamps. But all-weather machines have apparently been tried and found not beyond human ingenuity or American know-how. Ben Franklin certainly would have approved and might have been able to invent such a machine himself.

My communications with the Postal Department itself are not numerous. Occasionally I receive a card from them noting that they are holding something for me, with postage due; and after I spend some time and cab fare to get it, it turns out to be something I didn't order and don't want.

"AND WITH ANY LUCK WE OUGHT TO BE ABLE TO GET IT ACROSS TOWN IN A DAY OR TWO."
6/10/59

But if the Post Office Department has lately seemed chintzy about a lot of things, it has never been a Scrooge. Well before Christmas it sends me a cheery reminder to mail early and put my business letters in long envelopes. And when the holiday season and the holiday mail actually descend, the P.O. becomes literally expansive, taking on for the season additional employees like Santa Claus's little helpers. A Christmas tree complete with colored lights goes up outside the Post Office, and the lights burn late within. The delivery service is stepped up, and no trouble is spared to see that I receive—by or on December 25—those cards which bring me Season's Greetings from the Supercharge Garage and the Sixth National Bank of Cleveland. A letter I wait for and phone about might take three days to Zip from New York to Washington, but those impersonal greetings go through.

It is a jolly, bustling, merry time of year, and no one knows how to observe it better than old Postmaster General himself. He's never exactly asked what I'd like for Christmas, but when the holiday spirit is upon him, he might well like to know; and I'll tell him—better service when it's *not* Christmas. Greetings to him and all his assistants. And to all a good night—at a post office that stays open at night. ■

24. Outline

SIMON AND SCHUSTER, PUBLISHERS
ROCKEFELLER PLAZA
NEW YORK, N. Y.

GENTLEMEN:

With all the recent interest in novels and movies about politics, government and the military, I thought I might try something in that line, but maybe it's been done.

Of course you remember *It Can't Happen Here,* about a take-over by fascists; *All the King's Men,* about a Huey Long type character; and such recent stuff as *The Best Man, Seven Days in May, Dr. Strangelove* and so on.

What I thought would work up pretty well is a novel about the take-over of a major political party by a lunatic fringe. No armbands or any of that—just an assortment of people who have been on a consistent diet of anti-government stuff. You know—the goofball "educational" broadcasts of multimillionaire oil crackpots; the look-out-for-those guys-in-Washington material that's constantly put out in some papers and magazines; and of course the special tracts of fringe organizations, racist gangs and nut groups with their little "blue books" and "anti-red" pamphlets.

I'd need a central character to be a rallying point for all the kooks and all the simple people taken in by this kind of stuff.

The Huey Long type is out of date. And the way I visualize this guy, he'd be in politics, of course—a senator—but not a shouter and screamer. He'd be kind of a tougher-looking Warren G. Harding. He'd look like a good respectable businessman, probably a handsome, attractive, "sincere-looking" type. Matter of fact, I think he ought to have a business interest of some kind, and some kind of military background. Maybe a colonel or general in the reserves. That's kind of important, because while this guy wouldn't exactly represent the military-industrial complex, he'd be very high on the military.

The characterization would be fairly subtle—a combination of fool, phony and fanatic, leaving the reader to figure out how much of the junk this guy puts out he actually believes himself. And when he makes weird, conflicting statements, it wouldn't be entirely spelled out whether he was even conscious of what the hell he was saying from one day to the next.

This fellow says he's been around a lot, so he doesn't have to spend much time thinking. You know—like the old Kaufman and Hart play, where the movie mogul says, "That's the way we do things here—no time wasted in *thinking*."

There's a couple of simple ways I could delineate his character and views. First, his speeches and his record in the Senate, which could provide some good scenes—taking the floor to vote against civil rights, against anti-poverty programs, nuclear test ban treaties, against practically everything. Strictly an *anti,* with lots of emphasis on anti-Communism. The other angle is to have this fellow, or his ghost writers, put out some books, and give quotes from them.

They'd provide a kind of political blackstrap molasses and honey-and-vinegar product, laced with dynamite. You know those ads that say *YOU can release your HIDDEN SECRET POWERS! YOU can BEND OTHERS to YOUR WILL! Are you MASTER or SLAVE? YOU can TRIUMPH if you WILL it!*

That's our boy. But the *Hidden Secret Powers* of the individual and the states and everybody are being stifled by *The Government,* which is *Master*. And *The Government* is not using its own *Hidden Secret Powers* to crush *Communism*. The government of the country is no damn good. It's too strong at home and too weak abroad, and afraid to throw the Big Bomb around. See? He offers a combination of military adventurism and anarchy, but he calls it "conservatism."

Along with the bomb stuff, he tosses in some phrases about "natural law" and "the whole man," which are just vague enough to sound spiritual or something; and his followers eat it up. You've seen those funny signs: *I've Already Made Up My Mind. Don't Confuse Me With Facts.* Actually a coward about facing the facts of life in the world; but he compensates by saying the government is too cowardly to face the enemy. No McCarthy treason charges, though. He says the government hasn't got the WILL to TRIUMPH. And no rough stuff about impeaching the Chief Justice—but the Chief is a "socialist." So this guy's followers don't have any trouble getting the idea.

I mentioned *Seven Days in May.* But with this guy it's no military take-over. It's a giveaway. He says we're putting a lot of dough into training these military guys; they must know what they're doing; let 'em *do* it. If they want to use nuclear bombs, it's okay with him, and they don't even need to ask.

That's another angle. This guy complains about Federal authority but he doesn't mind military authority. To do a switch on the old Churchill phrase, he wants to become head of the Federal government to preside over the dissolution of the Federal government.

So how is he going to make it?

First of all, he's got going for him everybody that has a beef against the government, which is a lot of people. Anti-foreign aid, anti-spending-for-anything. And take the anti-Supreme Court guys alone—you've got the segregationists, the school prayer groups, the anti-reapportionment guys. And all the military types and the people who went for the soft-on-Communism stuff the last time around. This guy will take support from the Birchers, the Kluxers, anybody. His angle, which a new generation isn't going to remember from the old Mussolini days, is that anybody that's against Communism is okay. And don't forget the loners and misfits who go for his simple solutions and want to get in on Something Big.

Still, that's not going to be enough to put him over. Right? He tries out in a couple of primaries and doesn't do so well. But you know how many Presidential primaries there are in this country? Not so many. And you know how many convention delegates are selected without people knowing who's for what or how they're selected? Plenty. That's where this guy and his people make their big pitch. That's also where you find a lot of people who see voting rights and reapportionment coming in within a few years—and maybe even reforms in selecting convention delegates next. This guy is their last chance to head off democracy and roll back the Supreme Court and everything that's been going on the past thirty, forty years. He even wants to sell TVA. Never mind his talk about rolling back Communism in the world and using The Bomb. They figure about this stuff the way the Germans did about tough-guy proposals in 1932: "Responsibility is sobering"; and, "Tut tut, nothing is served as hot as it is cooked."

Anyhow, while everybody is watching the big primaries that made Kennedy, this guy is quietly making time at the crabgrass-roots level. And all of a sudden everybody wakes up to find this boy has almost got the nomination.

Now, here's something I think the readers will like—real newspaper people and recognizable politicians.

Doris Fleeson looks ahead and sees how this guy and his goons and young fanatics are taking over youth organizations. The guy himself calls Walter Lippmann, Joe Alsop and Roscoe Drummond radicals. Good thumbnail sketch right there.

Then I bring in characters like Ike, Nixon, Dirksen and so on—different names, but recognizable because they'll be caricatures of themselves. Everybody strictly himself but more so. For example, I'll have the Ike character backing and filling all the way. Urges everybody to run against this fellow. Then un-urges them and says this fellow is a nice guy, too. He's for everybody. Then he phones some attractive young politician to forgodsake stop this guy. Then he gets talked out of that and calls back to say, never mind, and include me out. Then he puts out statements that he doesn't want to stop anybody, and so on. It might seem like an exaggeration but you have to remember that this is the Ike who actually said in a television interview that in 1952 he didn't know what his brother and friends were congratulating him about when they jumped up from the TV set and whooped because he had just scored enough votes in the convention balloting to give him the Presidential nomination. And you remember how he said he wanted to phone Senator Taft and had to get someone to work the dial telephone for him because he didn't know how. So I don't think my Ike character will be too much of an exaggeration, and people will recognize who it is.

Same thing with Nixon. The old-new-new-old-every-which-way politician. He pats all the candidates on the back with a knife. Keeps looking for an almost-winner. Very friendly to our Anti-Government candidate, but hopes he'll break a leg at the finish line. Says he's neutral for everybody. When Big Boy finally has it just about wrapped up, the Nixon character says somebody should get in there and stop him—for Big Boy's own good! I think it would be a nice Nixon touch to have him say that the convention would make a better TV show if this guy is slowed down. Then he'll attack the guy that tries to stop Big Boy, and accuse *him* of vacillating. Then he'll say he wasn't attacking, he was just analyzing the young fellow's *problems*. And so on.

I could do this part with day-by-day quotes from the political characters, and provide a little humor there.

Now comes the convention. Don't get ahead of me and think I'm going to make it a horse race because I'm not. Big Boy has it cold. The whole story here is on the type of convention and the people there.

They won't be like major-political-party people—more like the old

Lemke-Father Coughlin-Gerald L. K. Smith crowds, if you remember those days. Very intolerant. More hate than hope. Anybody that's not for 'em is probably a Commie or a traitor. They push around some Negro delegates, rough up some radio and TV people, shake their fists at the press galleries, and shout down old-line decent guys who want the platform to come out against the Klan and Birchers and Communism.

They boo the Governor of New York, won't even let him finish a five-minute talk and holler for him to go home. He talks about the bomb threats he's received and the dangers of extremist groups. But the types he's talking *about* are the ones he's talking *to*—they've already taken over.

I don't figure to carry the story through to the White House and the nuclear button and the *On the Beach* ending. We wind up with a big convention scene where this guy accepts.

He makes a speech with the old blackstrap molasses junk in it, and the old anti-government, anti-Communist stuff. The guys in Washington don't want to *win* against Communism. And just to illustrate the old confusion and demagogy, this guy who is anti-Federal government comes out strong for keeping city streets safe, which is generally recognized as a local problem. This is in a speech accepting the nomination for President. But the real kicker is a line saying extremism is okay in a good cause. Wham! The extremists get the idea, and one delegate says, "We're going to have riots if we have to hire pickets to create them. And you know who'll get the benefit of those riots." That sums it up.

The movie prospects for this thing are great. We close with a shot of Big Boy looking strong and handsome and waving to the cheering delegates and gallery crowds. Here's this guy who prefers military to civilian control; who's been against civil rights legislation; who's never showed compassion for people less fortunate than himself; who's tied up with just about every shady political element from Joe McCarthy to George Wallace-racists; and whose big pitch is that he's against the Federal government. And the camera moves back to show hanging over him a big portrait of *Abraham Lincoln* on a banner that says OF THE PEOPLE, BY THE PEOPLE, FOR THE PEOPLE. And the delegates sing:

Glory, glory, hallelujah!
His truth goes marching on!

How's that for a finish? Of course this is just an outline. And as I said at the beginning, maybe it's been done. ■

I DO NOT PROPOSE
TO BECOME EMBROILED
IN ANY DISPUTE OVER
THE MERITS OF THE
BIRCH SOCIETY OR
ITS MEMBERS
— B. GOLDWATER
HERBLOCK

"WHY, SURE ENOUGH–IT'S FEARLESS BARRY HIMSELF."

12/22/61

"MIND YOU, I DON'T PUT IT EXACTLY THAT WAY."

11/21/61

CARRYING GOLDWATER ON BOTH SHOULDERS

10/6/63

"SORRY, OLD BOY, BUT YOUR WIFE AND I FEEL YOU'RE BECOMING AN EMBARRASSMENT."

3/6/62

BIRCHHEAD

2/20/63

"AS FOR CIVIL RIGHTS, I AGREE WITH SEN. GOLDWATER THAT THIS IS A MATTER OF STATE RIGHTS—UH—LET'S FINISH THIS SPEECH SOMEWHERE ELSE."

6/16/63

"YOU STAY OUT OF THIS!"

3/6/63

"THANKS A LOT BUT NO THANKS."
8/29/63

"NEVER MIND THE FINE PRINT, SON–HOW WOULD YOU LIKE TO WIN THAT GIRL?"
6/27/63

"WE OFF-LIMITS BOYS HAVE TO STICK TOGETHER."
8/2/63

"WHY SHOULD I DEBATE ROCKEFELLER?"

10/15/63

TUSK TO TUSK

6/25/63

"AS I WAS SAYING, THE ADMINISTRATION HAS FAILED TO TAKE A BOLD, FEARLESS STAND..."

7/24/63

"MAN, THAT LOOKS LIKE A REAL TWISTER."

9/19/63

"JUST AN EXPERIMENT, SENATOR— AT THIS POINT, ANYTHING'S WORTH A TRY."

2/11/64

"SO I SAID TO THOSE WISE-GUY KIDS, 'DO YOU KNOW OF ANYONE WHO IS LIVING IN ABJECT POVERTY . . .?' "*

3/6/64

"THAT'S THE TROUBLE DEALING WITH PEOPLE THAT CAN WRITE."

3/13/64

*Columnist Mary McGrory wrote of Senator Goldwater's appearance at Keene Teachers College, New Hampshire, in March 1964, ". . . The students had done their homework. The Senator had not done his. Nobody bothered to tell him that many of these scholars were lean and hungry hill folk who worked hard for their education.

"The Senator talked to them as if they were attending some country club college . . .

". . . A student pressed him as he kept urging private charity. Finally, out of patience for once, and genuinely baffled as to why the usual answers had been so badly received, he asked: 'Do you know of anyone who is living in such abject poverty that they are miserable?'

"There was an angry gasp in the audience. The boy said yes he did. . . ."

"HE SAYS THAT AFTER THE BLOODLETTING HE CAN BRING US PEACE."

11/17/63

"AS A LAWYER, I'D BE GLAD TO HELP YOU MAKE OUT A WILL."

4/16/64

"PARDON ME, DID YOU KNOCK?"

3/17/64

5/3/64

"INDIANA USED TO BE ONE OF OUR BEST TERRITORIES."

5/7/64

5/21/64

GREAT DEBATE

5/12/64

"YOU GUYS THINK *YOU* HAVE TROUBLE?"

5/6/64

"SEE–OUR MAN HAS AN ANTI-POVERTY CAMPAIGN TOO."

4/24/64

CALIFORNIA

5/29/64

"—MARRIED HER, HE DID, AND BOTH DIVORCED AND ALL..."
5/5/63

"I GUESS THEY FIGURE THIS KIND IS OKAY."
6/11/64

"WELL, NOW, THE WAY I LOOK AT IT, I DON'T THINK I OUGHT TO—UH—GET INVOLVED."
5/16/64

"ON SECOND THOUGHT, TURN BACK AND FORGET IT.
LET'S NOT BE PART OF A CABAL TO STOP ANYBODY."

6/10/64

"I WANTED TO MAKE SURE EVERYTHING WAS CLEAR."

4/10/64

"HOLD IT!"

6/30/64

6/17/64

"SHAKE HANDS–THIS IS A TIME FOR UNITY."

6/9/64

"GIDDAP, BOY–THAT'S A GOOD REPUBLICAN."

7/16/64

"WE WANT A CHOICE–*A CHOICE*– NOT AN ECHO–*AN ECHO*–"

7/15/64

AN AMERICAN TRAGEDY

6/5/64

"WE STAND UPON OUR HISTORIC PRINCIPLES–"

7/14/64

"HURRAH FOR THE–UH–
ELEPHANT WITH THE TUSKS ON
TOP OF HIS HEAD."
8/30/64

"ON ENDING VIOLENCE IN THE
STREETS–I THINK I'D CUT OUT
THAT PART ABOUT SMALL
TACTICAL NUCLEAR BOMBS."
9/7/64

"CALL A STAFF MEETING AT ONCE, AND TELL THEM
TO TELL ME WHAT TO SAY I SAID YESTERDAY."
8/24/64

Blairsville Junior High School
Blairsville, Pennsylvania